TURNING POINTS

TURNING POINTS

Stories of People Who Made a Difference

Max L. Christensen

Westminster/John Knox Press
Louisville, Kentucky

Unless otherwise indicated, scripture quotations are from the New Revised Standard Version of the Bible, copyright © 1989 by the Division of Christian Education of the National Council of the Churches of Christ in the U.S.A., and are used by permission.

Scripture quotations marked KJV are from the King James Version of the Bible.

Book design by Laura Lee

First edition

Published by Westminster/John Knox Press
Louisville, Kentucky

This book is printed on acid-free paper that meets the American National Standards Institute Z39.48 standard. ∞

PRINTED IN THE UNITED STATES OF AMERICA
9   8   7   6   5   4   3   2   1

Library of Congress Cataloging-in-Publication Data

Christensen, Max L. (Max LeRoy), 1919–
  Turning points : stories of people who made a difference / Max L. Christensen — 1st ed.
    p.   cm.
  ISBN 0-664-25357-1 (acid-free paper)

  1. Biography.   2. History, Modern—Miscellanea.   I. Title.
CT105.C43   1993
920.02—dc20   92-17831

DEDICATION

This book is a token of my gratitude for the blessings of hope and beauty that have flowed to me through the lives of our four children: Max Gordon and his wife, Janet Elizabeth; Mary Frances and her husband, James Martin Petrie; Timothy Allen; and Elizabeth Ann—and, of course, my wife, Barbara Brown Christensen, who wrote the first six words of the manuscript.

And special notes of appreciation are sent with love:

To our dear grandchildren: Justin James and Spencer Gordon Christensen, and Shelly Ann Petrie.

To my nephews, Christian Anthony and James Stephen Salak, and to the children of James and Nasrin, David Ali and Danaz June.

To John Joseph and Ann Louise Christensen and their children, Eric and Brandi.

To my honored namesakes, Max Allen Bachman, and the brothers Nils Christian and Max Hart Johnson.

And, not least of all, to poet Deetje Boler, my good right hand.

CONTENTS

INTRODUCTION

This is a book about hope—a collection of brief biographical sketches of certain notable men and women who, in moments combining crisis and insight, found the grace and strength to change our world for the better, forever. These divine taps on the shoulder, these stirrings of the soul, come in every time and place and form, in every race and culture, and at every level of human experience. They occur in calmly reasoned acts of will and in instant reactions to fear and hysteria; they appear in moments of joy and sadness, love and hate. These significant parts of our heritage are born in mystery. We cannot tell whether they come by chance or destiny, magic or impulse. We know for a certainty that great turning points come in response to the still, small voice of conscience, and we are equally certain that the voice of thunder will direct a turn.

A message of hope for the future came, for example, in a wildly beautiful vision/hallucination in the mind of a terribly hungover man in a drunk tank. Bill Wilson's dramatic moment brought, and still brings, sobriety to millions of alcoholics all over the world.

The future of freedom spoke one day in the harsh, grunting sound made by a stagecoach conductor as he cursed and yanked and pulled at the well-dressed Indian man, the young Mohandas K. Gandhi, who clung stubbornly to a luggage railing at the top of the moving coach. The ugly sound heard that day on the dusty South African road to Johannesburg marked the beginning of the end of British rule of India. Strangely, there was hope in the racist curse, "Nigger!" spat at Jackie Robinson who, though he did not know it, was being tested in a team manager's office in New York. He controlled his anger and maintained his dignity and changed

American baseball forever. And hope was in a horrified little boy's scream as he stood on a street in London and watched an old man being branded on the forehead with a red-hot iron shaped in the grimly prophetic letters: SS (Sower of Sedition). The cry of young Roger Williams, founder decades later of Rhode Island colony, carried in memory over oceans and years to become a shaping force leading to the guarantee of religious freedom in the Constitution of the United States.

There are quieter sounds—certainly more beautiful and equally enduring—such as those that were voiced one happy morning by Albert Schweitzer as his spirit suddenly overflowed with gratitude and reverence for the gift of life; we remember the great doctor-scholar-musician-missionary in the term "Africa's Saint." And there were the soft sounds of mothers weeping as they stood in a new military cemetery on a terribly scarred but now quiet battlefield. They grieved over the graves of their dead soldier-sons, killed only a few miles from the homes where they were born. Then, by a common, tender instinct, they began to place flowers over the graves of their sons—and on the close-by "enemy" graves as well. In this act of compassion and forgiveness, they called future generations to annual remembrances of the ultimate gifts of life made by our nation's patriotic youths.

Great shouts of glory and joy still come from the sacred hours when George Handel, an over-the-hill, dried-up composer, in an extended, almost feverish seizure of inspiration, gave to his community of believers a channel through which the praise of heaven has since flowed without ceasing.

What follows here is not a finely detailed study of great movements and complex personalities; it is, rather, a collage of special personalities—individuals who have given us pride of heritage, and the assurance, as poet G. A. Studdert-Kennedy has phrased it, that history will feel "the stubborn ounces of our weight."

WHY THIS BOOK?

Learned philosophers and scholars may argue over such things as whether a war was started with the first shot fired or whether it began, in fact, with flawed economic policies or poor ethnic attitudes or plotting arms dealers—or whatever. Looking at the big picture, they might say that life is a broad and complex continuum, and that no single person, alone, can stand in the way of a great movement whose time has come, or, for that matter, cause it to begin if the time is not ripe. Yet most would agree that great movements have leaders, and leaders must have moments when commitments are made, new attitudes formed, new directions chosen, and distant visions transformed into realities.

In this book, we will examine some important moments in the histories of great institutions and movements, and we will look at lesser-known occasions of splendid witness, which often pass without much notice. Here the adversary can be private grief, or a struggle with doubt or pain, sin or evil, or any of the dangers and threats that bring us so quickly to our knees.

A great many of the deeply personal moments we examine here may appear to have little or nothing to do with religion, as such, but there are others that can be described, appropriately, in the traditional vocabulary of faith. Some overly cautious writers, especially in the field of school textbooks, avoid entirely or make only the barest mention of religion because it might be considered a "touchy subject." This unnecessary widening of the gap between the secular and religious serves only to reduce significant spiritual experiences and moral decisions to trivia, and it strips them of the weight of importance they should bear. That is not good reporting and it is not good history. Our goal is to rescue some of these turning points so that they may be fitted more carefully and accurately into the complex and beautiful tapestry that depicts the adventuring human spirit. We will see that irrepressible force at work in the arts and sciences, in moral choices and ethical decisions, in social movements and politics, in public business and private prayer.

The Good Old Days of Today?

There is this reassuring possibility to be considered: We may be living in the good old days of today. In Roark Bradford's unforgettable play, *The Green Pastures,* one of the characters stands atop a knoll as the waters of the great flood described in ancient biblical literature begin to rise. All the familiar signs are being washed away. As chunks of the wreckage of a house he has known float by, he turns to a companion and says, "There ain't nothing tacked down; everything's done come loose."

There are many who interpret the present worldwide social turmoil as an ominous sign of the "beginning of the end." Before rushing off to seek safety in the arms of some modern Noah, they should listen to the calm voice of reason from a highly respected American educator. Professor John Bennett of Union Theological Seminary once recounted in a lecture certain evils that have been rejected one by one as peoples have learned over the centuries to place an increasingly higher value on human life. Mentioned in the distinguished professor's comments were such things as human sacrifice, the subjection of women, slavery, punishment without trial, dueling to kill, child labor, and the uncontrolled exploitation of men and women in industry and agriculture. To these could be added legal opium traffic, debtors' jails, confession by legal torture, murder of abnormal children by abandonment, the killing by desertion of old or incurably ill people unable to provide for themselves, and cruelty to animals. Some of these evils have not died entirely, to be sure, and some have lived on in only slightly less virulent forms, but the whole trend of history is against them.

That may be small comfort when we consider the increased complexity and danger of contemporary problems: drug abuse, AIDS, crime, political unrest, wars, racism, famine, poverty, the homeless, and the threat of nuclear holocaust. Serious anxieties arise when one tries to evaluate changing sexual mores and lifestyles, test-tube pregnancies, genetic engineering, damage to the ozone layer, the greenhouse effect, and the possibility of a deadly "silent spring" for our delicately balanced environment. The list is long, and the dangers posed to our civilization cannot be overestimated. Still and all, there has been no other time in the world's history when so many people were thinking and planning and working for peace. There has been no other time when so many people were engaged in the task of improving our health and environment. Creative impulses in church and state, in business and government, are being felt strongly, and the willingness to face change, however fearsome, was never firmer. "The good old days" are, or certainly can be, today. If we believe that, we have hope.

"THE BEST THINGS IN YE WORST TIMES"

Time spent in the company of great spirits will bring an awareness that some part of the beauty and courage in their lives has, in a lovely, even blessed way, become a part of ours. The process by which this enrichment of spirit takes place is a fascinating mystery to us—a little, perhaps, like falling in love. It is a lot like falling in love with the future. Robert Shirley did just that. The place was England, the year 1653. Church buildings were being desecrated and torn down, altars pounded to bits. Throughout the country lovely, irreplaceable stained-glass windows were being smashed. Puritans and other nonconformists, boiling with that peculiar, unfathomable form of hate that shows itself when religionists are at each other's throats, shouted cheers for their powerful leader, Oliver Cromwell, and set themselves to the task of the Long Parliament, an era of intolerance on the part of victors who—it must be remembered—had themselves been victims of the very same violent, unforgiving intolerance only months before.

Sir Robert Shirley, suffering anguish over the fact that the forms of worship he loved were outlawed, and heartbroken at the sight of many churches lying in rubble, took it upon himself to do what was for the times a very dangerous thing: He built a church. Cromwell, hearing of the new edifice, ordered Shirley imprisoned in the infamous Tower of London, where he soon died.

The church was described to me in correspondence some years ago as "still standing in Leicestershire—a modest, conventional and very beautiful place of worship." My attempt to locate and photograph the building while on a hurried visit to that city in 1990 was a failure, but the tribute, said to have been inscribed over the church's entrance, will endure:

IN THE YEARE: 1653
WHEN ALL THINGS SACRED WERE THROUGHOUT YE
NATION
EITHER DEMOLLISHT OR PROFANED
SIR ROBERT SHIRLEY, BARONET
FOUNDED THIS CHURCH
WHOSE SINGULAR PRAISE IT IS
TO HAVE DONE THE BEST THINGS IN YE WORST TIMES
AND
HOPED THEM IN THE MOST CALLAMITOUS

PART I

*Sensitive Spirits
and Caring Organizations*

BILL'S MIRACLE

Alcoholics Anonymous

This is the story of an event that has given us a giant, uniquely American rescue organization. Sir Robert Shirley, as we have noted, was a truly noble nobleman who paid with his life for the "crime" of building a church. William Wilson of this story was a drunk. Bill, as he was called, enjoyed alcoholism and atheism as much as the next fellow, which was not at all, but even so, he was not ready for the miracle when it happened. The place was a detoxification facility in a New York hospital where, as in times past, he had been brought for "drying out." The year was 1934, during the time of an extended national crisis known as the Great Depression.

The words "crisis" and "depression" suited Bill exactly. He was desperate in his desire to stop drinking but helpless against the craving; and the weight of depression lay heavily upon him. In a moment of what may have been terror or prayer—or both—he shouted: "If there is a God, let him show himself! I'm ready to do anything—anything!" The cry was scarcely off his lips when the light struck. The room, he said later, was suddenly filled with a luminous presence, which enveloped and penetrated his entire being. He felt purged and free—ecstatically so—and as the light faded away he was left with the certain feeling of an abiding presence, an inner peace.

Bill's atheism was so strong that for a time he struggled to dismiss the incident as a hallucination; but his wise physician, Dr. William D. Silkworth, assured him that a profound spiritual event had taken place. Members of the Oxford Group, a religious fellowship within the Moral Rearmament movement, were regular and helpful hospital visitors, and from a temporary association with them he learned,

3

among other things, of the therapeutic value of public confession. His renewed strength was such that he was soon able to return to his investment business, but more and more he felt called upon to share his victory with other alcoholics. While on a business trip to Akron, Ohio, he met an alcoholic physician, Dr. Robert "Bob" Smith. The two men, introduced to each other by a Methodist minister, Dr. Walter Tonks, discovered that as they tried to help each other, they were better able to deal with their own drinking problems.

This two-person fellowship, Bill Wilson (1895–1971) and Bob Smith (1879–1950), marked by a sustained, supportive interest and concern rather than preachments, soon began to enlarge and include other drinkers who had a real desire to achieve sobriety. Bill gave three-and-a-half decades of service to the organization, which continues today under the familiar name of Alcoholics Anonymous. Over the years, millions of alcoholics in 114 different countries have been helped through chapters now numbering more than 75,000. Though not professedly a religious organization, A.A. meetings include the saying of the Lord's Prayer, and the theological premise of a "power greater than one's self," however liberally interpreted, is basic to the A.A. Twelve Steps program of recovery.

Medicine, psychiatry, or spiritual advances may someday provide a means that will free men and women from the curse of alcoholism. Until then, as thousands upon thousands will testify, the aftereffects of Bill's miracle are waiting to be shared.

Any description of A.A. should include mention of a parallel yet independent organization, Al-Anon, which is composed of people who are not alcoholics. They band together in the A.A. style of simplicity and closeness to support each other in facing and coping with the problem of having an alcoholic spouse, family member, or close friend. Bill Wilson's wife, Lois, who died in 1988 at the age of ninety-seven, was of prime importance in inspiring and leading the flourishing and useful group.

A number of other individual and group therapy programs not associated with A.A. draw upon tested techniques to bring healing to persons suffering from drug abuse, compulsive eating, and other problems, thus extending the benefits of the organization in a variety of ways.

The Twelve Steps of Alcoholics Anonymous*

1. We admitted we were powerless over alcohol—that our lives had become unmanageable.
2. Came to believe that a Power greater than ourselves could restore us to sanity.
3. Made a decision to turn our will and our lives over to the care of God *as we understood Him.*
4. Made a searching and fearless moral inventory of ourselves.
5. Admitted to God, to ourselves and to another human being the exact nature of our wrongs.
6. Were entirely ready to have God remove all these defects of character.
7. Humbly asked Him to remove our shortcomings.
8. Made a list of all persons we had harmed, and became willing to make amends to them all.
9. Made direct amends to such people wherever possible, except when to do so would injure them or others.
10. Continued to take personal inventory and when we were wrong promptly admitted it.
11. Sought through prayer and meditation to improve our conscious contact with God, *as we understood Him,* praying only for knowledge of His will for us and the power to carry that out.
12. Having had a spiritual awakening as the result of these steps, we tried to carry this message to alcoholics, and to practice these principles in all our affairs.

The Alcoholic's Prayer

God grant me the serenity to accept the things I cannot change, courage to change the things I can, and wisdom to know the difference.

—Reinhold Niebuhr

---

*The Twelve Steps are reprinted with permission of Alcoholics Anonymous World Services, Inc. Permission to reprint and adapt the Twelve Steps does not mean that A.A. has reviewed or approved the contents of this publication nor that A.A. agrees with the views expressed herein. A.A. is a program of recovery from alcoholism—use of the Twelve Steps in connection with programs and activities which are patterned after A.A., but which address other problems, does not imply otherwise.

THE BANKRUPT SWISS BANKER

Jean Henri Dunant and the Red Cross

I t was a bloody business—but really none of his business—and the young Swiss banker who had traveled to Italy to discuss an important financial venture was tempted that day in 1859 to turn away from the ghastly spectacle of thousands of untended wounded and dying soldiers being carried into the town of Castiglione from the nearby butcher-battlefields of Solferino. But Jean Henri Dunant did not turn away. Instead, although he had no way of knowing it, he stepped at that moment into a curiously mixed life of fame, poverty, disillusionment—and immortality.

The French and Italians had combined their forces in an effort to drive Austrian emperor Franz Joseph and his soldiers from Italian soil, and on the day of the banker's visit to the French and Italian headquarters, casualties on both sides amounted to almost twenty thousand. Military medical facilities were completely swamped. Churches and homes in the city were jammed with the wounded and dying, and the streets were lined with wagons holding scores of groaning soldiers.

People lost in the pain and confusion of that day suddenly became aware of the commanding presence of a young man in a white business suit. Without any authority from the military the youthful banker began to organize effective emergency relief groups, and within a few hours some semblance of order was brought to the scene. To the surprise of most people, he insisted that the wounded be treated alike regardless of whether they were enemies on the battlefield.

In the months following the incident at Castiglione, he became increasingly interested in founding a voluntary, worldwide relief organization, and his efforts resulted finally in the formation of the

International Committee of Five. He succeeded, at Geneva, Switzerland, in 1863, in persuading the representatives of sixteen nations to adopt the principle that wounded soldiers and all medical workers be free from attack. It was agreed also that medical personnel and volunteers would not carry weapons. The symbol worn by the workers would be an identifying arm band—a red cross—a symbol that honored, in reverse colors, the flag of Switzerland.

This passionate interest in relief work caused him to neglect his business, and in a few years he was forced into bankruptcy. He lived in obscurity and poverty in the slums of Paris until 1870, when he stepped forward to lead relief work in the bloody and bitter days of the Paris Commune. After that he worked to persuade more nations to accept the principles that came, more than half a century later, to underlie the international rules for the treatment of prisoners and wounded as outlined in the Geneva Convention of 1929. He tried to persuade the relief organization, which by that time had come to be known as the International Red Cross, to interest itself in peacetime disasters as well as service in time of war. This principle was later accepted, but opposition at that time led him to again disappear from public sight.

In 1890 he was discovered living quietly in an Alpine village, and long-overdue honors—including, in 1901, the first award of the Nobel Peace Prize—began to come his way. His life (1828–1910) came to a close with his burial in Zurich, where he was laid to rest "as a simple disciple of Christ." As with all true disciples, his gift to humankind was compassion and mercy, and so long as people value these qualities the name of Jean Henri Dunant, founder of the Red Cross, will be immortal.

Clarissa Harlowe Barton (1821–1912), remembered by the more familiar name Clara Barton, founded the American branch of the International Red Cross in 1882. Earlier she had become known as a battlefield angel of mercy in European wars, and she carried the same respect in her own country during the Civil War. Crisis and disaster and wounded bodies were commonplace in her life, but she never lost the ability to minister to the wounded human spirit. An old friend, burdened by the painful weight of a long-held grudge, yet anxious to find a companion who would help him nourish it, reminded the famous nurse of a time years earlier when she had been the victim of a vicious act of hatred. When Clara acted surprised and unaware that such a thing had ever happened, the friend asked, "Don't you remember that?" Clara replied, "No. I distinctly remember forgetting it."

THE DIPLOMAT'S BLUFF

Henry Bergh and the SPCA

Henry Bergh, a dapper young diplomat, secretary of the U.S. delegation at the court of Czar Alexander II in Russia's city of St. Petersburg, leaned forward on the seat of his horse-drawn carriage and watched in anguish as an angry peasant standing a short distance away laid the whip again and again to a staggering, overburdened donkey. The pain Bergh felt as he watched the animal suffer was sharpened by the conviction that the man who was lashing the helpless beast was also degrading his own soul.

As a foreign emissary assigned to the then President Abraham Lincoln's delegation to Russia in 1863, he had no authority to stop the man, but he stepped down from the carriage and walked determinedly to a point between the man and the trembling animal and stood there with his right hand held high in a gesture that caused the peasant to drop his whip.

Bergh, after returning to the carriage, went over the event in his mind and tried to determine just what it was that had made the man stop, and he concluded that respect for authority had been the principal reason. The fact that he had no real power was beside the point—the peasant had thought of him as someone of great influence, and that had been enough.

When the wealthy career diplomat and man-about-town returned to New York some months later, he found himself becoming increasingly sensitive to the many acts of cruelty practiced upon animals by the population as a whole. Among the thousands of horses used to operate the city's streetcar system there were dozens of sick and lame animals that were whipped and forced to carry overloaded cars until they fell dead; dogs were used to operate window-display treadmills until they died of exhaustion; poultry was plucked live; gambling syndicates staged innumerable cockfights in which the roosters were equipped with metal slicing spurs; tubercular cows were supported upright by belly straps so they could be fed and milked until they died; and slaughterhouse operations were conducted in such a way as to cause needless suffering to the animals.

Bergh's belief that authority was necessary to curb cruelty led him in 1866 to call together a group of leading citizens and form what was soon to be known as the American Society for the Prevention of Cruelty to Animals. After great effort, the Society secured passage in New York that year of the first state anticruelty law, which, for lack of enforcement provisions, was almost ineffectual. Bergh, however, was moved to apply himself and his fortune to this job, and he stayed with it for the rest of his life. Public opinion was almost entirely against him at first, and newspapers delighted in describing him as a "meddler" devoted to the task of "preventing cruelty to cockroaches and bedbugs." However, as incident after incident was described in the newspapers, the tide of opinion began to turn in his favor. He also gave strong support to the founding of the Society for Prevention of Cruelty to Children.

The humane treatment of animals is now considered a natural and essential part of mature and ethical human conduct, and people now find it hard to believe that some of the extreme cruelties mentioned earlier were commonly practiced little more than a century ago. This fact itself is testimony to the effectiveness of the now worldwide Society for the Prevention of Cruelty to Animals, and its founder, Henry Bergh (1811–1888), the man who began a mighty crusade against cruelty when he stepped forward to place himself between an angry whip-wielder and a suffering beast.

THE LONG ANSWER TO PRAYER

George Williams and the YMCA

L ooking down through the mist at the dingy and crowded London street below, young George Williams watched from his room with mixed feelings of distress and compassion as the vague forms of his fellow dry-goods clerks passed through halos of yellow light around the street lamps. Now and again he heard the rasping voices of gambling-room shills and the raucous, shameless invitations of the streetwalkers.

George was one of the eighty clerks employed at Hitchcock and Company in 1841. They were housed in drab quarters in the upper floors of the store building, and, as in all other large business establishments of the day, they worked long hours. In general, they had little desire to spend their precious free time in wholesome pursuits. Williams had come from Bridgewater, a small town southwest of London, near Bristol, only a short time before, but already he was homesick and in need of friendship and decent, wholesome companionship. He would devote his prayer this night, he decided, to asking for one thing—friendship. Kneeling in lonely silence, he opened his heart to God.

Few prayers, one might surmise, have ever been answered more fully. Before a month had passed, J. Christopher (a name meaning "Christ-bearer") Smith, twenty-four, came to work at the firm and became Williams's roommate. Though Smith was four years older, the two shared many interests, including Bible study and prayer, and their room became a chapel for other like-minded clerks. The months rolled by, and Williams was the leading spirit at a meeting on June 6, 1844, when twelve young men decided to form a "Society for Improving the Spiritual Condition of Young Men Engaged in the Drapery and Other Trades." Two weeks later, at the suggestion of Christopher Smith, the title was changed to the "Young Men's Christian Association." Even the most optimistic among that original twelve—a significant number—marvelled at the rapid and vigorous growth of the movement throughout England, and they rejoiced in 1851 as chapters were opened in the far-off cities of Montreal and Boston, where growth was even more phenomenal.

The YMCA has continued to grow and mature and change. Today it ministers, as does the later-established Young Women's Christian Association, not only to youth—its original purpose—but to people of all ages and races, all denominations, faiths, and creeds in more than fifty countries. Through hotel, gymnasium, and school facilities, through recreational and religious study groups, the spiritual, intellectual, moral, and physical needs of men and women are ministered to in increasingly effective ways.

Sir George Williams (he was knighted for his work) was born on October 11, 1821. He died in 1905 certain of this one thing: God's answer to prayer never stops.

THE OLD ROPE TRAP TRICK

Robert Baden-Powell and the Boy Scouts

The usually hard-to-ruffle British general was more than upset about the incident; he was upside down over it—and he dangled there in midair, head downward, hanging from the rope that had somehow suddenly looped itself around his feet and jerked them skyward. The gardener working nearby who rushed to his aid assured him that a carefully concealed jungle rope trap is not the sort of thing one would usually be on the alert for in a quiet English park. "It's the young boys, sir," the workman explained. "They're all completely taken up with a new book on jungle war scouting, and they practice their tricks everywhere." The gardener, after cutting the rope, went on to explain that the book was written by a great English jungle fighter, Major General Robert Baden-Powell, hero of the 215-day siege of Mafeking during Africa's Boer War. The general thanked the man for his help, explained that he himself was Baden-Powell, and resumed his walk on that afternoon in 1900.

His mood was thoughtful. The scouts he had trained in Africa were part of a military machine—runners, spies, lookouts. What would be the effect of the book on these English lads? Would it not be possible to capitalize on this interest and yet direct their activities into more useful pursuits? The answer to his question did not come at once, but over the next few years, to the extent that his military duties would allow, he studied existing boys' groups and in 1906 devised a plan of his own. His group, though nonsectarian, would stress the moral as well as physical growth of boys. In addition to the healthy fun of outdoor crafts and activities, opportunity for the development of the individual's sense of honor would be given, and the qualities of initiative, alertness, and self-discipline would be sought. But that was not all. In a letter to a group he had established in Zuurfontein, Transvaal, Africa, he complimented them on their skill in crafts and on their good conduct, but added, "That is not enough. Do at least one 'good turn' for somebody every day."

In 1907 he conducted a two-week experimental camp for twenty boys at Brownsea Island, and in 1908 he formally launched the Boy Scout organization. In 1910, with the assistance of his sister Agnes, he founded the Girl Guides organization (the British equivalent of Girl Scouts) and, at the request of King George V, began to devote his entire time to the development of scouting.

Authorities differ on the exact details of the rope trap incident, but one thing is certain: The thanks of the world are due to the man who felt responsible for properly channeling the youthful interest he had aroused—the founder of Scouting, Sir Robert Stephenson Smyth Baden-Powell (1857–1941).

His grave marker is a small stone bearing the dates of his birth and death and a small circle with a dot in the center—Scout language that means "Gone home."

But there's more to the story. It happened one dark, fog-bound night in the city of London. Publisher William Boyce of Chicago tried to shrug off the vague sense of panic he was beginning to feel, and in a kind of assurance-seeking gesture, he reached out through the night mists to touch the cold and slippery street lamp beside him. It was hard to believe that he could be lost in the middle of a great city, and yet he was. He had heard some tall stories about the dense English fogs, but the thickness of the vapory shroud that now enclosed him was almost beyond belief.

He was startled at the sudden appearance of a gnomish form at his elbow, but relieved as the voice of a little boy came to him: "Can I help you, sir?" the lad inquired.

"You most certainly can!" replied Boyce, and he told the boy the address of the place he was trying to reach. Minutes later, after Boyce had been guided safely to his destination, he turned to thank the boy and offer him a coin. The thanks were graciously accepted, but the boy declined the tip by saying that he belonged to a group of Scouts who made it a rule to do a good turn for someone every day without thought of reward. Before the visiting publisher could think to ask his name, the lad had disappeared into the fog.

When Boyce returned to Chicago later that fall in the year 1909, he gave the incident publicity in his newspaper, and soon, with the help and leadership of many other Americans, interest in scouting was aroused in the United States. On February 8, 1910, a congressional charter was given to the group.

As is the case with most doers of good deeds, the helpful English lad probably never knew the profound effects of his simple act of courtesy, but millions of his fellow Scouts know the story. They have caused a monument to be erected in the International Boy Scout Training Center at Gilwell Park in England:

> To the Unknown Scout whose
> Faithfulness in the
> Performance of the Daily
> Good Turn brought the
> Scout Movement to the
> United States of America.

THE PROTESTANT MONKS

Roger Schutz and Taizé

Protestants are not well known as monastery founders—the record indicates, in fact, that they get around to starting one about every four hundred years. Yet Roger Shutz (b. 1915), a Swiss theological student, had the vision of a "new" kind of monastery that would witness to the Christian will for unity, and in 1940 he organized and became the prior of a small band of men who shared his dream. Four years later a permanent home for the group was established in Taizé, France. It is said to be the first Protestant monastery since the Reformation (not including, of course, the Anglicans or Orthodox). Members of the Taizé Order, as the community is now called, numbered about sixty-five at the end of the group's second decade. They had come from twelve different countries and represented twenty denominations and three communions.

The monks have taken lifetime vows of poverty, chastity, and obedience, following ancient practice, and they meet three times a day for prayer. There is, however, no atmosphere of retreat from the secular world. On the contrary, engagement and social action occupy a large part of the order's time. When the brothers are working in the village or engaged in some service or building project away from the monastery, they wear ordinary working garb. Within the monastery compound, they wear a simple white alb or cloak over their work clothes. They share in the heavy monastery farm chores and work at other things—woodcarving, architecture, ceramics, or whatever—according to their time and talent. Worship forms are changeable and generally informal, but they use certain printed liturgies from a variety of religious traditions when they are moved to do so.

The members conceive of themselves as missionaries and sometimes travel many miles from Taizé, but they make no attempt to "buttonhole" or "break into" the lives of others. Instead they stand ready to offer Christlike service to those in any kind of need—spiritual or material. The late Pope John XXIII, hearing of their work, called the brothers to Rome and blessed them for bringing about what he called "this little springtime." May they continue to flourish, and may their harvest be "truly plenteous."

Members of the Taizé Order appear to heed this advice in St. Benedict's Rule from the year A.D. 525:

> If any Pilgrim Monk shall come from distant parts with wish to dwell in the Monastery, and will be content with the customs of the place; and does not by his lavishness disturb the Monastery, but is simply content; he shall be received for as long as he wishes.

> If, indeed, he shall find fault with anything, and shall expose the matter reasonably and with the humility of charity, the Abbot shall discuss it with him prudently less perchance God hath sent him for this very thing.

> But, if he shall have been found contumacious during his sojourn in the Monastery, then it shall be said to him, firmly, that he must depart. If he will not go, let two stout monks, in the name of God, explain the matter to him.

THE PATIENT BELL

William Booth and the Salvation Army

If at Christmastide you marvel at the patient ringing, ringing of the small hand bells by the plainly, quaintly attired members of the Salvation Army, you may wonder how it all started. In the words of the Army's founder, this is what happened: "From the day I got the poor of London on my heart, and a vision of what Christ could do for them, I made up my mind that God should have all there was of William Booth."

General Booth (1829–1912) was born in picturesque Nottingham, England, and was converted to Christianity at the age of fifteen. He was a lay preacher in the Methodist Church for a time and later moved to a London mission. When he found that his converts were not being accepted in the "respectable" congregations, he began to organize the Salvation Army.

"A man may be down, but he is never out," said Booth, and what soon became five million members of his Army in ninety-eight countries gave ample proof of that. From the beginning they found no one too lost, no place too dark, no work too difficult, and no sacrifice too great. A high church official, when asked his opinion of the Army, replied: "I don't like it at all, but I am afraid God Almighty does."

Booth had married a Quaker woman, and their union was blessed on Christmas morning, 1865, with the birth of Evangeline, named for the Evangel, or Gospel. She grew to be a hardy, tomboyish girl who enjoyed high diving—a fairly unusual talent for her generation. She began her work at sixteen by visiting the lowest saloons, prisons, and alleyways. When the White Angel, as she came to be called, entered a place she would start to sing just any sort of familiar song, and when the people became quiet, she sang a hymn. She ministered with music, as people in the Salvation Army still do, because, as she said, "music makes people remember the good that is in them." For years she lived in slum rooms among those she had undertaken to help. Though often attacked by angry mobs, she persevered, and in later life headed the world organization of the Salvation Army for six years.

The bells ring at Christmas for food and shelter, for the down and out, for the homeless, for rehabilitation, for clothing, for medicine—and they ring because God "got all there was" of William Booth and his family.

His approach to life is eloquently expressed in what may be the shortest Christmas holiday greeting on record. At one point he wanted to send a cablegram to each of the Army's many outposts, but was faced with the problem of expense. After thinking about it a bit, he was able to get his message across in this one-word cablegram which he sent to all his posts: "Others."

THE GARBAGE INSPECTOR

Jane Addams and Hull House

Most well-bred young women would not be especially happy or excited to win the title "Garbage Inspector," but Jane Addams of Chicago's famed Hull House showed more delight over that honor than she did over any of the several other awards—including the Nobel Prize—that came to her in later life.

Born September 6, 1860, in Cedarville, Illinois, Jane Addams gave early signs that she would be somehow set apart. As a child of six, while riding with her father in a carriage through the poor section of town, she told him that someday she would "build a great big house and invite the poor people to come in."

After a good education that included study abroad, she visited Toynbee Hall in London, the world's first social work center, and was so inspired by what she saw there that she determined to establish some similar work in the United States. Months later, in Chicago, while searching the West Side slums for a house that could be made into a service center, she found a run-down mansion that had been built in 1856 by a man named Hull. She rented a portion of the building (the Hull family later gave her the whole block), and with the help of a friend, Ellen Gates Starr, she set about cleaning it up. Then, twenty-three years after her girlhood promise, she invited the poor people to come in.

The term "social worker" was as yet unheard of, and her neighbors were at first suspicious. Moreover, Jane Addams had only vague ideas about what she really hoped to accomplish there. Within a few weeks, however, young mothers of the area were coming to Hull House at tea time to receive informal instruction in child care. Other neighbors made the happy discovery that the bathtub at Hull House (the only one in the vicinity) was available for their use. The sick and hungry found a refuge, and youngsters found a place to study. People of all races and cultures came to find a common meeting ground at Hull House.

The hardships of life in the slums in 1889 are almost impossible to picture. Sewage lay in the muddy streets, garbage was left to rot in alleys, and running water was scarce. Disease, delinquency, and suffering were everywhere.

Jane Addams began a one-woman campaign to see that sanitation laws were enforced and condemned buildings torn down. Ward politicians and businessmen, who had at first tolerated her as a harmless do-gooder, turned against her, but pressure from the newspapers led to her eventual appointment by the mayor of Chicago as Garbage Inspector. Heartened by this moral victory (which brought immediate improvement to conditions), she gave vital leadership to other causes: child-labor laws, desegregation of the races, world peace projects, sanitary codes, public playgrounds, nurseries, and industrial safety.

American presidents and thousands of other important citizens gave many honors and awards to Jane Addams during the nearly fifty years she lived and worked at Hull House (she died in 1935)—but the famous Garbage Inspector was usually too busy to give them much notice. Scrub brush in hand, she was hard at work keeping Hull House clean and ready for "the poor people to come in."

MANSION HOUSE 9000

Edward Chad Varah and Suicide Hot Lines

This bombed-out London church of St. Stephen Walbrook might very well be the answer to his prayer, thought the Rev. Edward Chad Varah as he carefully picked his way through the rubble-choked parish office that November day in 1953. He had accepted the call to become rector of the barely functioning St. Stephen's because of the church's central location behind Mansion House, the lord mayor's dwelling—and also because of its small membership, only twenty-five persons. For years he had nourished the idea that from such a parish as this he could apply himself to alleviating one of London's most serious problems: suicide.

At the beginning of his ministry, he recalled, there had been the young girl of fourteen who had committed suicide after ignorantly mistaking the signs of female maturity for a dread social disease. Just a word from an informed person could have prevented that tragedy. There had been many other instances through his ministry in mental hospitals, prisons, and slums, where the right word from the right person at just the correct moment could have saved a life. People really didn't want to do away with themselves, he felt. It was only that hope was gone, and society, like the priest and Levite in the New Testament parable of the Good Samaritan, had "passed by on the other side" without caring. Some, perhaps most, suicides had been caused by the bitter loneliness one often encounters in a large city. Others had resulted from a lack of religious faith, and still others from mental imbalance.

The suicide rate in London, he had been shocked to discover, averaged one person every eight hours, every day of the year. Many of these deaths could have been prevented, he believed, if only those tempted had been able to turn to some friendly listener. No one in London was ever very far from a telephone, and the thought had occurred to him that if there were a widely advertised telephone service that distraught people could reach for friendly counsel in time of emergency, the frightful rate might be substantially reduced. The one emergency telephone number known to all Londoners was 999, dialed for police, firemen, or ambulance service. If he could get a number something like that—Mansion House 9000, for example—perhaps some desperate people would want to call it instead of committing that most final of all acts. What London needed was a Good Samaritan who would listen sympathetically and then try to help the injured person back to a happier life.

As he stood looking around the room, his glance fell upon a dust-covered telephone which had apparently lain untouched there since the great London blitz of World War II. He reached over and picked up the instrument and was surprised to find that it was still "live." On impulse, he dialed the operator and asked if it might be possible to have the number changed to Mansion House 9000. "What number are you calling from, sir?" inquired the operator. Varah rubbed quickly at the discolored dial plate and then stood erect in amazement—the number printed there was clearly legible: Mansion House 9000.

Varah interpreted this "coincidence" as a sign of God's approval of his plan. He moved quickly to advertise the number and then organize the now famous Samaritans of London who cooperate in maintaining a twenty-four-hour vigil at that telephone. The tweedy, bespectacled Anglican rector soon had the assistance of more than a hundred volunteers, many of whom he had saved from suicide, and he won the support of psychiatric and social workers as well.

The idea quickly spread. Samaritans formed branch organizations in many other British cities. A Lutheran organization sponsored a like movement in Germany and Sweden. Catholic groups were formed in Vienna, Frankfurt, and other cities. In New York City, desperate persons could telephone the Save-a-Life League. Distressed persons could call Rescue Incorporated in Boston. Most cities now have similar hot line programs. Edward Chad

Varah, born in 1911 and still going strong in the 1990s, is convinced that the world's suicide rate could be cut drastically if there were telephone Samaritans in every community. There is no evidence to either support or refute such an optimistic assumption, but those who work in the field have no doubt that their efforts are steadying and saving many, many lives. And, as in all cases, the ministry blesses the minister.

THE CHILDREN'S CRUSADE

Clyde Allison and UNICEF

The Rev. Clyde Allison, pastor of Bridesburg Presbyterian church in Philadelphia, wasn't thinking of producing any Nobel Peace Prize winners on that particular Sunday night before Halloween nearly fifty years ago. He was only trying to devise a means whereby the youngsters of his congregation could collect a little money during their trick-or-treating for children in famine areas. As it turned out, his little plan eventually produced several million honest-to-goodness little Nobel winners, and some of them may have rung your doorbell on Halloween. Pastor Allison (born in 1917 and now retired) had heard of the then newly established United Nations International Children's Emergency Fund, an agency created in 1947 as a temporary replacement for the United Nations Relief and Rehabilitation Agency, which had been dropped some months after World War II ended. A little money had remained in the treasury of the older U.N. branch, and officials had decided that it should be spent for the relief of sick and hungry children in war-torn countries who were still suffering after only two years of peace. It would be a good idea, the pastor thought, to supplement the U.N. money in a small way and at the same time let the members of his Sunday school have the experience of helping other children.

Two decades later, UNICEF, as it came to be called, had become a permanent and essential part of the U.N. structure, and the "Trick or Treat for UNICEF" practice was taken up by thousands upon thousands of churches, schools, service clubs, and other organizations. In 1965 the Nobel Peace Prize was given to UNICEF—the first time in the history of the Nobel awards that the prize was given to a group rather than an individual. Thus, every child who participated in UNICEF shared in the honor of the award.

By the time UNICEF reached its twenty-fifth birthday, the Children's Fund had provided assistance in child welfare in 137 countries. Nearly 400 million children were given vaccinations against tuberculosis. Some 415,000 children were cured of leprosy. More than 425 million children were examined for yaws, a contagious tropical disease, and 23 million were treated. About 71 million children were examined for trachoma, an eye disease leading to blindness, and 43 million were treated. UNICEF had equipped 12,000 large health centers and 38,000 smaller centers in 132 countries—along with several thousand hospital, pediatric, and maternity wards. Some 2,500 teacher-training schools and 56,000 associated primary and secondary schools received UNICEF equipment. A thousand prevocational training schools for young people were equipped, as well as thirty-one training institutions for instructors. Aid had been given to 3,000 women's groups and 2,500 day-care centers. Some 3,000 child-care centers, youth clubs, and orphanages were aided. In nutrition programs, over 9,000 school gardens and canteens were assisted.

These figures were compiled more than twenty years ago. In spite of the agency's ever-broadening outreach to the sick and needy and in spite of the important work done by other charitable organizations, this challenge, as described in a recent UNICEF bulletin, still remains: "*Every day,* measles, whooping cough and tetanus, all preventable through an inexpensive course of vaccines, kill almost 8,000 children. *Every day,* diarrhoeal dehydration, which can be prevented for pennies, still kills almost 7,000 children. *Every day,* pneumonia, which can be treated by low-cost antibiotics, kills more than 6,000 children."

UNICEF aid was, and is, given in response to requests by responsible government officials of *any* country in amounts consistent with the degree of need. UNICEF, like the U.N. itself, deals with people—the hungry, the sick, the illiterate, the untrained—and gives them a chance to help create a better life for themselves.

Hungry persons are angry persons. Stable, satisfied populations are not as likely to start wars or revolutions. The interdependence of life in our world today is such that everyone, at one time or another, is affected by the programs of international cooperation. Who, then, needs UNICEF? We all do.

The UNICEF Prayer for Children

Now I lay me down to sleep;
I pray Thee, Lord, the souls to keep
Of other children, far away,
Who have no homes in which to stay,
Nor know where is their daily bread,
Nor where at night to lay their head,
But wander through a broken land,
Alone and helpless—Take their hand.

STAMPING OUT DISEASE

Einar Holboell and Christmas Seals

Postal clerk Einar Holboell sighed as he looked around the cluttered Danish post office and saw the familiar signs of increasingly heavy Christmas mail as the holiday season of 1904 drew closer. It was not so much the thought of hard work ahead that bothered him as the knowledge that there would be so many sick and suffering children unable to share in the joys that the oncoming flood of packages would bring. The problem of sickness among children had always been a particular concern to the kindly Holboell, and he wished that he might somehow help them.

It was then that a great thought occurred to him: Why not, while the holiday spirit of giving was strong, ask people to buy inexpensive Christmas stamps or seals to decorate their packages and letters, and then use the profits to help sick and needy children? A penny wasn't much, but there were lots of packages, and perhaps in time the stamps might earn enough money to build a special hospital for children.

Holboell had no difficulty in selling his postmaster on the idea, and within a short time the King of Denmark himself called upon his people to support the plan. Warm-hearted Danes were quick to respond, and funds sufficient for the building of a fine tuberculosis hospital were soon in hand.

One of the Christmas stamp-bearing letters from Denmark was addressed to Jacob Riis, a Danish-American writer who was later to achieve fame as one of America's greatest journalists. Riis wrote a magazine article in which he told of the success of the Christmas stamps in Denmark, and urged their use in fighting the disease in this country. Riis himself was no stranger to the tragedy of tuberculosis—six of his brothers had died of the disease. The sincerity of his plea caught the heart and imagination of thousands.

The National Tuberculosis Association of America, which was in the process of formation in 1904, adopted the Christmas seal plan in 1907 at the suggestion of Emily Bissell, member of a prominent family and cousin of a pioneering physician who was a leader in the treatment of tuberculosis. With the help of Philadelphia's leading newspaper, the American public joined wholeheartedly in the battle against tuberculosis among people of any age.

It would be hard to estimate how many lives have been saved through what has now broadened into one of history's noblest health crusades—for the stamp sale now benefits disease prevention, health education, hospital care, and rehabilitation—but we can be sure that millions of people are grateful to the Danish postal clerk Einar Holboell (1865–1927) for the part he played in "stamping out" disease.

THE HIGH COST OF LYNCHING

Laurence Clifton Jones
and Piney Woods School

A speaker at a fund-raising affair does not usually have to cope with the problem of a tightening noose around his neck, but this occasion was different. It was not, in fact, intended to be a fund-raising event at all—it merely turned out that way. In the beginning it was your regular 1930s-style lynching party, and all that stood between Laurence Clifton Jones and the tightening of the hangman's loop around his neck was a five-minute speech about the school he had founded, the Piney Woods Country Life School near Jackson, Mississippi. Jones had been grabbed by the "vigilantes," dragged from the little church where he had been speaking, and charged with "radical agitation" because they had heard that his speeches in the vicinity had caused much interest and comment. It did not matter to them that the comment, among both white and African American people, had been favorable. Like any lynch mob, all they needed to know was that a "nigra" was speaking and people were listening. That was enough.

Yet the cold-blooded, impatient nature of the lynchers did not prevent them from allowing the customary "few last words." The little congregation remained at the church, praying intensely and hoping for a miracle, while, without fear and standing straight, Jones told his captors how, after graduating from the University of Iowa in 1909, he had come to Mississippi to bring education and practical training to members of his race. With a worldly fortune amounting to a dollar and sixty-five cents, Jones had sat down on a pine stump in an open field and started to teach three illiterate boys to read. He had worked as a farm laborer to support himself, and the school, aided by small gifts of land and money, had soon grown to be an important community asset. Jones, a believing and practicing Christian, did not beg for his life—he told of his work. After a few minutes, two leaders of the hanging party stepped forward and removed the noose. Then, in silence, they took up a collection from those assembled, placed the money in the teacher's hand, and disappeared.

Half a century later, the prospering school owned about two thousand acres of land, which together with buildings and educational equipment was valued at several million dollars, and had an enrollment of more than 350 students. The school has sent out to rural communities many hundreds of trained farmers and agricultural experts and has trained additional thousands in a variety of skills ranging from housekeeping to auto mechanics to shorthand. Graduation ceremonies at Piney Woods are unusual. Each student, before receiving a diploma, must prove his or her mastery of the skills learned at the school; and their exhibits thus range from a well-cooked cherry pie to a teaching credential to a demonstration in the art of calf vaccination. The school runs today very well without the personal oversight of its founder, but the hardy, self-sacrificing, and industrious spirit of Laurence Clifton Jones (1884–1975) lives on as a vital part of the school's tradition. Many gifts, some of them quite large, have come to Piney Woods Country Life School, but none has equaled in importance that handful of money given by the shamefaced lynchers who started out to a hanging party but found themselves instead participating in a fund-raising campaign.

THE ENCOUNTER

William Colgate and Colgate Charities

The deckhands had finished their job of unsnarling the lines of the canal boat, and the captain, standing on the smooth towpath that ran along the edge of the steep bank, made ready to jump back onto his vessel. As he stepped back casually to eye the distance he brushed against a young lad who had approached unnoticed, and the captain paused to smile an apology. Something about the youth—perhaps his serious, clean-cut face—caught his attention. As they chatted briefly he learned that the boy, whose name was William, had been apprenticed as a candle and soap maker, and had come at age twelve from a poverty-stricken home in Kent, England, to find employment here in America. Sensing William's anxiety over the future, the boatman suggested that they kneel and pray for guidance. When they arose the boy was feeling better, indeed, and the captain left him with this advice: "Be a good man; give your heart to Christ; give the Lord all that belongs to Him of every dollar you earn. Make an honest soap, give a full pound."

William pondered these things carefully as he walked on toward New York, and he resolved to do his best in following the stranger's advice. Later, after establishing membership in a tithing church, he found employment, and after working hard to save money, he started his own candle and soap business. As the endeavor prospered, he quietly increased his giving to church, education, and charity and finally devoted his whole income to those causes.

He never reached sainthood, and never claimed it, nor was he better intentioned than millions of children before and since; but credit is due, certainly, to William Colgate (1783–1857), whose name a university now bears. His brief encounter and prayer with a stranger led to the founding of the famous soap company—and, eventually, to one of America's great philanthropic and educational endowment systems.

THE PATRON SAINT OF PLAY

Joseph Lee
and the National Recreation Association

The dirty little urchins of Boston in 1894 were free to prowl in the streets and alleys the clock around, and they could bully one another on the sidewalks to their hearts' content; but when they started playing baseball in the streets—well, that was too much, and the police were quick to arrest them. That was the way things were for slum children in those days, and most people were willing to let it go at that. But there was one man, an aristocratic young banker named Joseph Lee, who, after reading the account of one such arrest, threw down his newspaper in disgust and declared that the children had been "arrested for living." Determinedly, he made his way to the city's tough South End and began to look for a place that could be converted into a playground. Within a few days he had secured permission to use a junk-littered vacant lot, and he set to work clearing it of debris.

Later, as he watched the happy children participate in the games and contests he had organized, he knew that he had found his niche in life. Play was a natural and indispensable part of childhood, he mused—a basic human right—and he would devote himself to seeing that it was enjoyed by all children. The whole of his time and fortune was dedicated to the improvement and enrichment of life for children—especially underprivileged children. He organized athletic leagues, tournaments, music festivals, and pageants that benefited thousands of Boston children. Lee, a Harvard graduate who had studied law, engaged in court battles that won for children the right to play games on Sunday. His efforts to get young lawbreakers tried in courts separately from adult criminals led to the establishment of the Juvenile Court of Boston. Special services for sick and learning-disabled children were, at his insistence, instituted in local schools. He suggested and provided initial financing for the Harvard Graduate School of Education—a remarkably progressive educational achievement for his time.

In later years he led in the organization of what eventually became known as the National Recreation Association, and he served as its president for twenty-seven years. In World War I he received the Distinguished Service Medal for his attention to the recreational needs of servicemen. Many high honors came to Lee during his lifetime (1862–1937), but his greatest reward came simply in watching happy children at play. Out of their wholesome endeavor would come, he knew, some of the traits and qualities essential to full and useful lives. Because of this insight, the man who protested "arrests for living" will be remembered as the patron saint of play.

THE DAY THE DEVIL SAT DOWN
AND CRIED

Dwight Lyman Moody
and Moody Bible Institute

It was a difficult and trying moment for the ruler of the Kingdom of Evil—and when it was all over, the Devil sat down and cried. The place was a shoe store in Boston, and the year was 1855. Edward Kimball, a Sunday school teacher, had been a little troubled about one of his pupils, an amazingly successful young shoe clerk who was not taking his religion very seriously. On impulse, Kimball decided to stop in at the store and lay the matter out in black and white. The strong-minded youth was not one to be buffaloed, but he listened courteously to Kimball's interpretation of life as something headed either up to heaven or down to hell. Only, said Kimball, by a decisive conversion and a spirit-filled life could a man find purpose in this world and peace in the next. All this was very familiar language, but then Kimball concluded with a challenge that jabbed the young man's spirit wide awake: "Today's world has yet to see what God can do with, and for, and through, and in a man who is fully consecrated to Him." The story of shoe clerk Dwight Lyman Moody's attempt to meet that challenge is one that would make the angels rejoice—and Satan weep.

Moody was born in Northfield, Massachusetts, on February 5, 1837, the son of poor parents who were unable to provide him with much schooling. He was a busy mischief-maker as a child, but upon reaching manhood he learned to apply his energy and enthusiasm to his work. Some months after his conversion, he moved to Chicago, where he rented a shack in the slum section and started a Sunday school, which grew, within two years, to fifteen hundred students. He worked among thieves and guttersnipes, and soon in "Little Hell," as his district was called, there was a prospering, useful church. Moody's physical vigor and endurance were incredible: He would often make two hundred brief pastoral calls in a single day—actually running from place to place in the tenements at top speed—and he buttonholed nearly every stranger he met to ask, "Are you a Christian?"

In 1870 he became acquainted with Ira David Sankey, a tax collector with a fine talent for music, and the two men joined their particular gifts to create a new method of mass evangelism. Moody's business knowledge and genius for organization, coupled with a sharp understanding of the values of music and showmanship, resulted in mammoth services in which as many as five hundred ushers were used and choirs numbering fifteen hundred singers assembled. He was a powerful speaker, and what he lacked in good grammar he made up for in sincerity.

Millions of dollars poured into the Moody campaigns in the United States and England, but he kept almost nothing for himself. The greater portion of the money was used to found or support educational projects—among them the now famous Moody Bible Institute in Chicago—and the balance was distributed to the needy. The great evangelist and revival leader died in 1899 after bringing happiness and blessings to thousands. It was commonly said of Moody that he reduced the population of hell by a million souls, but he always chuckled at that suggestion, for, while he believed in hell, he was much more interested in heaven—and that, perhaps, is the reason Satan cried.

THE VISITING NURSE

Lillian Wald and Visiting Nurses

T he head of the family, a badly crippled professional beggar, had left the "apartment" earlier for his daily stint of soliciting pennies. The other eight people who lived in the two filthy rooms of the tenement house in New York's East Side slum district were on hand, though, that day a hundred years ago to stare at nurse Lillian Wald as she stood hesitantly in their doorway. In one corner of the room, she could see a woman lying on a dirty, blood-soaked bed. Other members of the family sat on rickety chairs or squatted against the battered walls. The child who had interrupted her earlier in the day, during her class in care for the sick at the nearby teaching center, stood across the room by a sickbed, beckoning her to enter.

Most women of her genteel background would have been inclined to turn away from the dismal, heartbreaking scene, but Lillian Wald was no ordinary person. She had chosen nursing as a career at a time when it was not considered a proper endeavor for cultured women, and she had, moreover, agreed to come and work in an area where "her kind" of people were never seen. The teaching sessions had been real eye-openers, but this miserable and tragic real-life situation was a challenge to her very soul.

Crossing the room quickly, she took one careful look at the hemorrhaging woman and sent the boy for a doctor. Then, after bathing the woman, she set about cleaning the room. Hours later, though greatly upset by the event, she left the place thinking that if people were told of these conditions they would rally to help provide home nursing services for the great host of poor people from every racial and religious background. But she was due for another shock: Most of the people she talked to were willing to accept this kind of suffering as "part of the nature of things." With the exception of her own mother, who gave what she could, Lillian Wald was able to find but little support as she started her work. Iron-willed determination and day-by-day sacrifice made the difference, however, and finally one Jacob H. Schiff was moved to give her regular and substantial backing.

Many obstacles arose as she worked to accomplish her dream of bringing competent nurses to assist the underprivileged. She lost some financial backing in her not-very-private war against sweat shops and child labor, and she was ostracized in some quarters for her "radical" views on the right of women to vote; yet withal, the Henry Street Visiting Nurse Service she established in 1893, the first of its kind in the world, prospered and grew and serves to this day. Similar services have been established by various groups in cities all over the world, and they are accepted now as essential to community life.

Most of the millions of sick people who have benefited from the unique idea and ministry of Lillian Wald (1867–1940) have never even heard her name, but they see her still whenever a visiting nurse appears at the sickroom door.

PART II

Great Souls of Great Movements

THE YOUNG BOY'S VOW

Roger Williams and Religious Freedom

It was no place for a little boy, but he was too sick with fear and horror to run. He was too shocked to think clearly, yet a vow to fight bigotry and intolerance was forming deep within him.

The street crowd in London on that day so many years ago watched with the boy as the old clergyman in the pillory was lashed brutally again and again. One of the frenzied tormentors lunged forward with a knife and slashed off one of the prisoner's ears. Another smashed and split the victim's nose with a heavy club. Then, in a sudden and heavy silence, still another stepped forward holding a white-hot branding iron. The crowd gasped as he pressed the hissing iron against the old man's forehead. He drew it away then, revealing the deep, bloody letters "S.S." The aged cleric was indeed a "Sower of Sedition," for he had dared to believe and preach in a way not approved by the established church.

An intense individualist, the boy eventually came to North America, where, as a clergyman himself, he became a champion of religious tolerance. In 1636, after being banished from Massachusetts for his views, he founded the settlement of Rhode Island and established the town of Providence, creating an island of safety in troubled days, a place where honest seekers would find the principle of religious tolerance honorably maintained. Quakers and many others under persecution elsewhere found a home here. A maverick religionist by most definitions, an ardent believer in democracy and liberal government, Roger Williams (1603?–1683) strongly influenced the form of the United States Constitution and its Bill of Rights more than a century before it became the law of the land.

We remember the boy who remembered his vow: Roger Williams, apostle for religious tolerance and understanding in the United States.

THE BLACK ALTAR

Elijah Lovejoy and Freedom of the Press

The Rev. Elijah Lovejoy clenched and unclenched his fists that November day in 1837 as he listened to the angry shouts of the mob outside the warehouse where he had determined to make his stand. He blinked nervously as an occasional bullet crashed into the side of the building, and he turned now and again to look at the newly uncrated printing press that stood near the center of the room. It was shiny, inked, and clean—and it was, he thought, a kind of glistening black altar upon which he would soon, perhaps, have to lay his life.

But there was more at stake than just one life and one printing press. He had come here to Alton, Illinois, after being pressured out of St. Louis for editorial views expressed in the little Presbyterian journal, *The Observer,* he had published there. Two other mobs had destroyed other presses because he had insisted upon the right to publish his opinions against slavery. Four days earlier, he had addressed a violently prejudiced town meeting called by those who tried to silence him by continual harassment. He had challenged them to name any law he had broken, and they had been unable to answer. He had left the meeting with these words, "If civil authorities refuse to protect me, I must look to God; and if I die, I have determined to make my grave in Alton. I have sworn eternal opposition to slavery, and by the blessings of God I will never turn back. With God I cheerfully rest my cause. I can die at my post but I cannot desert it."

But it was one thing to talk about the possibility of death at a town meeting where only words were flying; it was quite another to face the fact of death here among the flying bullets. A simple announcement to the crowd that he would stop the editorials would save his life. He was a young man, only thirty-five, and he could move to another, safer place and continue the battle there.

Looking across the room he could see his brother, Owen, a minister of the Congregational Church, crouching against a heavy packing case. As their eyes met, Elijah knew what he must do. There would be no turning back—the issue would be faced here and now.

Moments later a single, hate-sent bullet took the life of Elijah Parish Lovejoy (1802–1837), the man John Quincy Adams described as "the first American martyr to the freedom of the press." Owen survived the wild wrath of the destructive mob and later became a member of the U.S. Congress, where he was a strong supporter of Lincoln in the abolition movement. He devoted himself fully to the cause for which his brother gave his life.

Elijah's death, widely commemorated at the time, did much to awaken the American conscience. Thanks to the contribution of Lovejoy and many others, the principle of freedom of the press is now firmly established in our democracy. American journalists have caused bronze markers to be erected at the place where he died, but a more fitting memorial comes to you every day in the unfettered editorial columns of your newspapers where thoughtful writers work to keep alive the vital principle for which he died.

PIONEER OF THE SOUL

John Woolman and Human Rights

S ome pioneers are challenged by the thought of a new life in a distant land; others, who live in the world of great and new ideas, become pioneers without ever leaving home. John Woolman, though he did considerable traveling around the American colonies in the pre-Revolution days, is remembered primarily as a pioneer in the world of ideas concerning human rights.

Woolman, a Quaker farm boy, was born, it is thought, on October 19, 1720, in New Jersey. He showed no special spiritual or intellectual talents until he was a young man. Then, experiencing a deeper conversion to the faith in which he had been raised, he began what was for many years a virtual one-man campaign to eradicate the social evils of his day. Even his Quaker friends, whose social thought and conduct generally could be considered above average, were left far behind by Woolman's "radical" ideas.

The radical farm boy thought, for example, that human slavery was contrary to the will of God; many Quakers, pious as they were, held slaves. Further, most people in the colonies thought of poverty, among people of any color, as a somehow necessary evil in every society. Woolman's challenge of this popular notion upset many leaders of the time. The modest, self-effacing reformer held what was then considered the curious notion that the Native Americans in the area had full ownership rights to the land on which they lived, and he shocked many by saying that their hunting grounds were being stolen. He protested vehemently against the practice of giving or selling rum to them, especially when the signing over of their lands or possessions was involved. He felt strong inward drawings to preach the gospel of Jesus Christ to Native Americans, and for this he was subject to much ridicule. In short, the gentle humanitarian looked at all people, rich or poor, of whatever color, as unique and important creations, children of God—valuable in their own right and for their own sake.

John Woolman's first breakthrough came within the ranks of Quakers when he persuaded many of them to free their slaves. For years he traveled about the colonies preaching wherever people would listen, and he managed at the same time to write many books and articles that still survive and are read to this day. *The Journal of John Woolman,* which is included in the Harvard Classics and in Everyman's Library, provides a compelling description of his travels. Great social movements must necessarily be developed by a few pioneers of the soul. Woolman (1720–1772) was one of these few.

YET ANOTHER ROOT OF REFORM

William Wilberforce
and the Antislavery Movement

T he purpose of a vacation, according to the likeable young politician's past experience, was to rest and recover from the effects of one year's carousing to get ready for another. On this autumn night in 1784, however, as William Wilberforce prepared to leave the luxurious southern coastal "playground" of France and return to his work as a member of the English Parliament, he felt that he had somehow come to possess a new and very different kind of strength, but he was not quite certain as to how it could be used.

Earlier in the year, the twenty-five-year-old "man about town" had on impulse invited his one-time schoolmaster, Isaac Milner, to accompany him on his vacation. The two men had engaged in long conversations on the subject of religion and had read together for hours in the Greek New Testament. As they moved carefully through the accounts of the life of Jesus, it had seemed that he was reading the Gospels for the first time. Feelings of guilt and shame that he experienced at first soon began to disappear, and he was suddenly aware of a profound sense of peaceful assurance and power within.

In this state he had tried to review and evaluate his life. The picture had been painfully clear: Except for a stunted body prone to illness, he had been blessed with—and had wasted—most of the things that a man could desire: intellectual brilliance, wealth, and social position. Beginning now, he resolved, this waste would stop.

The story of William Wilberforce's use of his life from that day forward is one of the most inspiring chapters of English history. Within three years he took up a position of leadership among the then small and weak antislavery forces and worked for more than forty years for the passage of the now famous Emancipation Bill. He had many followers and admirers in the United States, and it would be hard to overestimate his influence on and his ties to the antislavery movement in this country. In addition to the renowned legislation (which became law a month after he died), he devoted his time and fortune to such things as work among the blind, the improvement of clergy education and living conditions, the founding of a Christian newspaper, the expansion of the British Bible Society, and the support of books and publications designed to promote religion. Four of his sons led distinguished careers in church, education, and government.

William Wilberforce (1759–1833) possessed no great physical strength, but he found in the New Testament the power to lead others in lifting the burden of bondage from the backs of millions of slaves.

AN AUDIENCE OF ONE

John Newton and the Experience of Grace

The fear-sickened English sailors who clung to the hatch covers of the storm-tossed vessel *Greyhound* did not know whether the screaming demand to God uttered by their young fellow crewman, atheist John Newton, was meant to be a curse or a prayer, and Newton himself could not have told them. He had been thrown from his bunk moments earlier when a smashing wave had stove in one side of the ship, filling his cabin with icy water. After crawling through the dark passageway and on to the quarterdeck, he watched in terror as bits of the ship's cargo of dyewood and beeswax spewed forth from the jagged hole.

As the slow minutes passed on that day in 1748, a strange question began to form in Newton's mind: How could he pray to, or for that matter curse at, someone in whom he did not believe, whose existence he denied? His whole adult life had been built around the proposition that there was no God, no purpose, no morality in this purely material and sensual world. He had left the fanatical religious ideas of his parents when he went off to sea as a boy of eleven and had in later years eagerly embraced the ideas of the freethinkers of his time. Wherever possible, he had outdone them. If mild immorality was their fashion, then gross immorality was his goal. If foul language was their weakness, then obscenity became his rule. That he had succeeded in his quest for soul sickness was not to be doubted—he had lost his previous job on a dirty slave ship because his manner and bearing were too foul. Now, in this moment of danger, he had heard his own unsophisticated soul cry out. What did it mean? It meant, he decided, that it was time to face up to the issue his panic had raised: his beliefs about God. Through what the crewmen described as a miracle, the dyewood and beeswax cargo proved sufficiently buoyant to keep the ship afloat, and as the storm waned the ship made its way to a place of safety.

John began what was destined to be a fruitful exercise of his poetic talents in religious poems, but he did not reach the goal of religious maturity immediately. In 1774 he wrote one of his now famous hymns, "How Sweet the Name of Jesus Sounds on a Believer's Ear," while sitting on the deck of a slave ship, the hold of which was filled with moaning slaves being carried to Charleston, South Carolina. There were other problems as well. As he began to show an interest in religion, his neighbors in Liverpool were surprised when he, a slave trader (not a thoroughly disreputable occupation in his day), began to associate with members of the then highly disdained Methodist movement.

His long, uncertain journey toward conversion—not helped much by the fact that several thousand slaves were sold to American clergy—moved a giant step nearer completion in a remote country chapel in England one wet, foggy evening. The minister who had come to officiate at the service was agitated by the fact that, after traveling a long distance on foot over rough terrain in foul weather, he found the chapel completely empty except for a stranger who sat in a rear pew. His clothing indicated that he was a seaman or dock worker. He did appear sober, however, so it would be foolish, the clergyman decided, not to hold the service after coming all this distance. With all appropriate dignity, then, the visiting minister walked quietly across the chancel to the prayer desk. Omitting nothing, he concluded the lessons and prayers and moved to the pulpit for the sermon. As he began to preach it occurred to him that his "congregation" would certainly have no reason to think that the gospel message was intended for somebody else, and he was pleased as the sermon progressed to notice that the young man was paying most careful attention.

After the close of the service, Newton got up from his seat at the back of the church and approached the minister to ask if he might have the benefit of further counsel. Upon receiving the preacher's warm assurance that he would be glad to stay and talk, Newton poured out the degrading story of his life as a deserter from the Royal Navy, his subsequent career as a slave trader, and the taint that he felt lay upon his poetic gifts. The clergyman listened patiently and then began to speak quietly of God's loving forgiveness and grace. Soon Newton was able to sit up straight and smile. A terrible weight had been lifted.

John Newton (1725–1807) eventually found his calling as a pastor-poet in the Church of England. His fresh and vigorous sermons at St. Mary's Woolnoth in London attracted huge congregations, and he is remembered as well for several books of poetry and prose. Many of his hymns are still popular today, especially "How Sweet the Name of Jesus Sounds," "Glorious Things of Thee Are Spoken," and "Amazing Grace."

Newton, who died at eighty-two, preached to many large assemblages during his ministry. He was never much impressed by numbers, however, for he remembered with thanks that most important of all days, when he himself was an audience of one.

A DIFFERENT KIND OF MINISTRY

Jacob August Riis and the Social Conscience

It was the year 1876, and the Rev. Dr. Ichabod Simmons, having given one kind of advice in a public sermon, in the privacy of his study found himself in the curious position of having to give the opposite counsel to a young Danish immigrant who had come to him for guidance. On the preceding Sunday, Simmons had issued a strong call for men to give themselves to the ministry, and the eager, open-faced young Dane who sat now before him had responded to the plea. There was no doubt in the clergyman's mind as to the youth's suitability for the ministry—he was clean-cut, alert, intelligent, and sincere.

In the course of their discussion, Simmons learned that the inquirer had been born in Ribe, Denmark, the son of a professor of Latin who had wanted him to stay in the world of scholarship. The boy's adventuresome spirit, however, had prompted him to come to the United States. He had arrived in New York penniless and without friends in 1870 and for several years following had supported himself by doing carpentry and other odd jobs. His natural talent for languages soon enabled him to master English, and he eventually found permanent employment as a reporter on the New York *Tribune*. It was in this work that he had been brought face-to-face with the mammoth evils of crime and poverty in the city, and his pursuit of the ministry was based on his desire to help solve these critical problems. It seemed, then, to Simmons that the youthful reporter had already found his "ministry," and as he placed his hand on the young man's shoulder in a gesture of warm encouragement, he dismissed him with these words: "Follow God's call wherever it leads you. But my conviction is you will serve the Lord better not by becoming a minister, but by staying in the newspaper field and bringing about reforms. I pray that if you do, you may have great power."

Power was the word for it. The newspaperman, Jacob August Riis, followed the clergyman's advice and began a one-man crusade that eventually shook the city of New York to its foundations. In article after article, and in many books, he aroused the public to demand action on such varied problems as the slums, police corruption, impure drinking water, and inadequate playground facilities. After working for about ten years on the *Tribune,* he spent another decade as a writer for the New York *Evening Sun* and then retired from journalism to enter directly into the work of slum clearance.

Unlike some reformers, Riis was a man of happy countenance, and it was clear to all around him that the inspiration for his work sprang from a simple, joyful love of country. Theodore Roosevelt once called him "the ideal American citizen," and historians credit him with having pioneered in the development of the nation's social conscience. In the late summer of every year many communities observe "National Newspaper Week," and in thoughtful discussions of the place of newspapers in national life, the name of Jacob Riis (1849–1914) is often heard. He is, in fact, sometimes referred to as a "saint" of journalism. Though Riis himself would laugh at it, the term is not far wrong. He had great faith in the power of prayer, and he believed mightily in the concept of God as companion and guide. He always found time to be with his children, and he led his family in weekly Bible-reading sessions. The words of poet-clergyman Philip Doddridge (1702–1751) well describe the ministry of Jacob Riis:

> Thy face, with reverence and with love,
> We in Thy poor would see;
> O may we minister to them,
> And in them, Lord, to Thee.

TOO BUSY TO WRITE

Harriet Beecher Stowe
and Uncle Tom's Cabin

Many a construction project has been delayed while kindly workmen waited for fledgling birds to fly away from a nest in a tree due to be cut down. This is the story of how history waited while a baby fussed. "As long as the baby [her seventh child] sleeps with me at night," the young mother said in a letter to her brother, a minister, "I can't do much at anything, but I will do it at last. I will write that thing if I live." It could be said that the restless infant delayed for a time, at least, one of the most significant pieces of American literature, but it was bound to be written.

The precocious daughter of famed Congregational clergyman Lyman Beecher, Harriet was born June 14, 1811, in Litchfield, Connecticut. One of her first compositions, written at the age of eleven, was titled, "Can the Immortality of the Soul Be Proved by the Light of Nature?" At fourteen she was profoundly moved by a sermon preached by her father, Lyman Beecher, and she pledged her life as a follower of "the Way." Later, as the wife of a low-salaried young college professor, she was encouraged to continue in her successful writing career, and she did so to the extent that family obligations would permit.

Her six brothers were ministers; one of them, Edward, was a leader in the growing antislavery movement. Again and again he asked that she use her talents in behalf of the emancipation campaign, but the answer was always the same: "Too busy." The subject was much in her heart, however, and during rare moments of quiet she reflected on how she might serve. The day came when her ideas crystallized, and, putting aside housework and sleep, she went to work. "The story almost wrote itself," she said later. She worked far into the night, writing the final pages on rough grocer's paper when the supply of manuscript sheets was gone.

Her book, subtitled "Life Among the Lowly," was first published on June 5, 1851. It was a tremendous success and quickly ran through dozens of printings in serial, book, and play forms. Its effect in arousing public opinion against slavery was immeasurable. We remember the book by the more familiar portion of its title, *Uncle Tom's Cabin,* and we remember the housewife and mother, humanitarian and author—Harriet Elizabeth Beecher Stowe (1811–1896).

"WHILE GOD IS MARCHING ON"

Julia Ward Howe
and the "Battle Hymn of the Republic"

There was a peculiar, uncertain mood in the nation's capital that night. Julia Ward Howe, a poet of some reputation, arose from her bed, finding it impossible to sleep. The Civil War had just begun, and newly recruited troops were pouring into the city from the north and west. Looking down from her room in Willard's Hotel, she watched in silence as they marched through the dim patches of light cast by street lamps. They were not soldiers—they were plowboys and clerks, salesmen and book-keepers. They marched awkwardly, singing with forced enthusiasm the song "John Brown's Body," which had been set to an old revival-meeting tune. Looking off into the black night she could see the scattered, luminous dots of many campfires where men lay huddled together against the cold.

She had come from Boston to Washington with her husband, Dr. Samuel Gridley Howe, a member of the Sanitary Commission who had been sent to look after the health of the volunteers from Massachusetts. (Dr. Howe, incidentally, is remembered as the first physician to attempt the education of a child who was both deaf and blind. He succeeded in educating Laura Bridgeman, who later became a teacher of Annie Sullivan, the woman who led Helen Keller out of silence and darkness.) As Julia Howe returned to her bed she found herself humming the marching song that drifted up from below. Her pastor, the Rev. James Freeman Clarke, who had accompanied the Howes on the trip, had asked her earlier to use her poetic gifts in composing a different, more inspirational set of words to the tune, and she had agreed to try—but not so much as a single line had come. She thought about this for a while and then, finally, prayed herself to sleep.

It was still dark when the sound of marching awakened her, and she realized suddenly that the verses she had sought were forming in her mind. Quickly taking a piece of Sanitary Commission stationery (now on display in the Library of Congress), she wrote the poem that within a few months gave the Union Army a strong new sense of purpose and determination as it touched and braced and lifted the heart of every man:

Mine eyes have seen the glory of the coming of the Lord;
He is trampling out the vintage where the grapes of wrath are stored;
He hath loosed the fateful lightning of His terrible swift sword;
His truth is marching on.

Refrain:
Glory! Glory! Hallelujah!
Glory! Glory! Hallelujah!
Glory! Glory! Hallelujah!
His truth is marching on.

I have seen Him in the watch-fires of a hundred circling camps;
They have builded Him an altar in the evening dews and damps;
I have read His righteous sentence by the dim and flaring lamps;
His day is marching on. (Refrain)

He has sounded forth His trumpet that shall never call retreat;
He is sifting out the hearts of men before His judgment-seat;
O be swift, my soul, to answer Him: be jubilant, my feet!
Our God is marching on. (Refrain)

In the beauty of the lilies Christ was born, across the sea,
With a glory in His bosom that transfigures you and me;
As He died to make men holy, let us die to make men free!
While God is marching on. (Refrain)

—"Battle Hymn of the Republic"
Julia Ward Howe, 1819–1910

THE FIGHTING QUAKER

Susan B. Anthony and Women's Liberation

A merican Quakers, also known as the Society of Friends, have made valuable contributions to our heritage both in terms of personal piety, which they have sought as individuals, and in consecrated peace efforts, which they have made as a group. Yet one of their most important "contributions" to our heritage was a prayerful and energetic woman named Susan B. Anthony, who started, waged, and won one of the longest and noisiest battles in history. The battle was waged not with weapons, but with words and ideas, and the contending forces were—as they have been from time immemorial—men and women.

Susan was born at Adams, Massachusetts, in 1820, the daughter of a "radical" Quaker who encouraged his daughters to sing at their work. In Quaker homes of that day, mothers were given an equal place with fathers, but as Susan grew up she realized that elsewhere the laws of the land made the husband the unquestioned master of the home. He owned all family property, including his wife's money and clothing. Women could not vote, act as guardians of their children, serve on juries, or work in any of the professions except music and teaching. They were generally forbidden any education beyond elementary school. People seemed content to have things that way, and attempts to introduce changes were treated harshly by men and women alike. In 1848 Susan heard of efforts by Elizabeth Cady Stanton and Lucretia Mott to gain legal and political rights for women. After meeting with these leaders, she quietly resolved to dedicate the rest of her life to the struggle for equality for women. In the course of her fifty-eight-year crusade she may have given more public addresses and been pelted more often with rotten eggs and vegetables than any other woman in history. Her faith in the essential rightness of the cause was supported by prayer and daily Bible reading, and because of it she was able to endure jeers and insults, financial distress, and even jail.

Two decades passed before the first breakthrough came: the passing of a law in New York that allowed married women to control their own property. Shortly after that came the news in 1869 that women had been granted the right to vote in the Territory of Wyoming. With exasperating slowness, other states began to follow suit, and the tide of public opinion began to turn in her favor. She lived to stand before cheering crowds while high officials, including presidents, praised her work in women's liberation long before that term was ever used.

The right of all women in the United States to vote was finally achieved on August 20, 1920, when the universal suffrage amendment to the Constitution was ratified. Many of the other political and legal rights for which she worked have been written into the various state constitutions. The war between men and women may not be over yet, but if and when a peace treaty is ever concluded between the two, we can be assured that women—thanks to the efforts of Susan B. Anthony (1820–1906)—will have had their chance to vote on it.

THE ANGEL OF NEWGATE

Elizabeth Gurney Fry and Prison Reform

Her new pink shoelaces and purple shoes seemed to be more than a little out of place at a Quaker prayer meeting, the visiting American preacher declared; and he kept on declaring it through what turned out to be a two-and-a-half-hour sermon. Betsy, thoroughly embarrassed, squirmed impatiently through the early part of the Friends' Meeting at Goat's Lane in the English countryside. As the service on that Sunday morning of February 4, 1795, wore on, however, she found herself admiring the speaker's sincerity. What he said about the need for Christian discipleship was true, she conceded, and that evening fifteen-year-old Elizabeth wrote in her diary, "I know now what mountain I must climb. I am to be a Quaker."

The "mountain" was easily scaled. Betsy soon took her place among the Friends and several years later married one of their leaders. She found her calling first in establishing schools for poor children in London, where she had moved; she also founded a greatly needed charitable nursing order. But a chance suggestion by a fellow Friend that she interest herself in improving conditions at Newgate Prison led to the work for which she is best remembered.

She was shocked on her first visit there in February 1813 to find 190 women and 100 small children (though mostly innocent, they were forced to come with their mothers or be left in the gutters to starve) crowded into one small, filthy section of the jail. There was no segregation as to types—the young first offenders, the old, hardened criminals, the insane, the innocent children—all were dressed in rags and huddled together along the spike-studded walls. No prison official dared to enter the section without a heavy guard, but Elizabeth Gurney Fry (1780–1845) walked in alone one memorable day and, standing in the center of the yard, explained that she was a mother wanting to help other mothers. After a brief chat, she led them in prayer and Bible reading. In later visits she established classes in reading, Bible study, sewing, and money-earning handicrafts. Within a few months the ward was changed from a place of bedlam to one of peaceful activity and order.

The dramatic change wrought by the Angel, as she soon came to be called, was admired by farsighted prison authorities all over Europe. Useful jobs gave or restored to many prisoners a sense of security and dignity; segregation of types of offenders reduced the spread of criminal ways within the prison; the practice of extreme cruelty and humiliation was greatly reduced. The battle is far from won, but if victory comes it will be partly because an angel wearing pink shoelaces knew what mountain she had to climb.

THE PIONEER PHYSICIAN

Elizabeth Blackwell

There is a point at which the pressure of opinion of friends and loved ones becomes too much to bear, and on November 7, 1848, Elizabeth had reached it. At first they had laughingly scoffed at her desire to become a doctor. Later, when it had become apparent that she would not give up her ambition, their mood changed to one of bitter disgust that anyone who called herself a lady would be willing even to consider such a physically intimate profession. She almost wished she could change her mind and be freed from this increasingly lonely independence. Moreover, the prospect of medical school filled her with terror—she was not at all sure that she could successfully complete the training, and there was great doubt whether anyone would recognize her as a physician if she did. Even with the hearty support of her friends the way would be difficult, and without that support or any hope of it the future seemed bitter indeed.

She thought it was the strangest irony that her desire to help humankind's physical suffering could lead to this utter agony of mental despair. "O God," she whispered, "help me, support me. Lord Jesus, guide me, enlighten me." Her whole being went out in this yearning cry for help, and suddenly, overwhelmingly, the answer came. "A glorious presence, as of brilliant light, flooded my soul," she wrote later in her diary. "There was nothing visible to the physical sense, but a spiritual experience so joyful, gentle and powerful surrounded me that the despair vanished." This moment of ecstatic prayer opened the way for women in the practice of medicine, and Elizabeth Blackwell (1821–1910) became the first woman doctor of medicine in modern Western history. The English-born achiever who had come to this country as a child entered the

Geneva Medical School of Western New York and later opened a private dispensary that in 1857 became the New York Infirmary and College for Women. Returning to England in 1869, she became professor of gynecology in the London School of Medicine for Women.

The entry of women into this heretofore restricted field was, of course, inevitable, and if Elizabeth Blackwell had failed in her endeavor, someone else would have come along eventually to make the breakthrough. Her own sister, Emily, took a medical degree just six years later. But history lays the honor upon this woman who entered the profession with the noblest prayer-grounded motives and ideals. The example she made for those who follow in her way has proved a blessing to us all.

THE RELUCTANT MISSIONARY

Ida Scudder—Doctor in India

How much pressure is required to change the mind of a young woman who is determined never to become a missionary? This much: the deaths, on a single night, of three women in childbirth. Ida Sophia Scudder (1870–1960), the daughter of a medical missionary, was born in India and sent to the Dwight L. Moody School for Girls at Northfield, Massachusetts, where she determined, among other things, that she was not at all inclined to the missionary field. In 1894, when Ida was twenty-four, she was called back to India because of the serious illness of her mother. One night shortly after her return, a worried Brahmin came to her door and asked that she come and assist his wife in childbirth. Ida knew nothing of such things and told the man that he should speak to her father, the doctor. The Brahmin refused, saying that his religious belief would not allow him to have a man near his wife when she delivered. There was nothing that Ida could do but send him on his way. By the strangest of coincidences, two other men came that same evening, one a Muslim and the other another high-caste Hindu, seeking the same assistance. In each case she offered her father's services and was refused. In each case the man went away grieving. Greatly troubled, she spent the night in prayer, and on the following day she learned that all three young wives had died. Her decision was not long in the making: She would enter the Woman's Medical College in Philadelphia (now Medical College of Pennsylvania) and study medicine so that she could, within a few years, return to India and help prevent similar unnecessary deaths.

Five years passed quickly, and she returned as a doctor at the Union Missionary Medical College at Vellore, India. The great need for any kind of professional medical help in India made her life a blessing from the start. Beyond that, she was able to enter and minister in many homes where male doctors were forbidden. Over the years, she delivered many thousands of babies and developed special skills in the handling of difficult births. The college, a cooperative endeavor supported by eleven denominations, soon elevated her to the position of teacher, and though she remained an active practitioner, she was able at the same time to train hundreds of desperately needed doctors and nurses.

The once-hearty spirit of reluctance became only the faintest memory as she told her classes: "You are going out, not only to cure diseases, or to assist in the delivery of babies, or to teach mothers how to care for their children—but to live close to Christ, to follow in His footsteps in going about doing good, and to hold up Christ as the only help for a sinning, sorrowing world."

MEANWHILE, BACK AT THE POND

Henry David Thoreau,
an Independent Thinker

Henry was not the first man in history to violate openly one of the Ten Commandments, but he was one of the few who prayed that others would follow his example. The commandment he rejected so thoroughly was the one that declares: "Six days you shall labor. . . . But the seventh day . . . you shall not do any work." He taught that the order of things ought to be reversed—six days of rest and one of labor. Henry David Thoreau, American philosopher and master of the art of simple living, made a career out of doing only the things he wanted to do. A teacher, tinkerer, and outdoorsman, he was admired by those who knew him well as a wise man and philosopher. Among his friends was poet Ralph Waldo Emerson, who provided him with lodging in his home.

On July 4, 1845, Thoreau retired to a small hut he had built beside Walden Pond near Concord, Massachusetts, and for the two years following spent his time thinking and writing and enjoying a close and gentle companionship with God's wild creatures of the forest. Whenever he needed a few cents to buy food that he could not raise or prepare himself, he worked in town just long enough to pay for it. Henry had his own ideas about taxes. He was jailed once for refusing to pay his poll tax, and he was so angered over this that he wrote an essay titled "Civil Disobedience." Mohandas Gandhi later studied the article and spoke often of the influence it had on his philosophy. The Rev. Martin Luther King, Jr., in our time also made effective use of the ideas contained in the essay.

Emerson liked Thoreau very much but thought he had gone to extremes in refusing to pay taxes levied by President Polk to support the Mexican War. While visiting his friend in jail, he sighed, "Henry, Henry, why are you here?" "Mr. Emerson," Thoreau replied, "why aren't you here?"

Thoreau was not primarily a social reformer, however. He was a cracker-barrel philosopher who had the same message for every individual he met: "Rest. 'Lay not up for yourselves treasures on earth.' Cultivate quiet. Live simply. Do not struggle for wealth. Be free." He hated cities, factories, railroads, slavery, and whiskey. He loved solitude and the out-of-doors.

His skill in logic never brought him to the point that he could see that mines and steel mills were necessary to provide him with a good ax, something he considered an absolute necessity in this life. And perhaps, in view of the curious way he lived, we could call him eccentric. Looking at the matter in another way, though, we can observe that there are already enough people in this world who know that we must have steel mills in order to produce axes—we need Thoreau (1817–1862) to tell us that we need quiet and simplicity, too.

THE BEGINNING OF AN END

Mohandas Gandhi and Nonviolence

The slender, immaculately dressed, dark-skinned young lawyer who was perched alongside the driver of the now-halted South African stagecoach struggled to contain his anger as he looked down at the dirty cloth the conductor was spreading over the footboard. "Here, Sambo," growled the conductor, looking up at him, "you sit down here. I'm coming up next to the driver and have me a smoke."

The young man's hands fingered nervously at the brass rail along the coach top, tightening firmly as he replied: "You seated me here, though I should have been seated inside. That insult I put up with. Now you want me to sit at your feet. I refuse."

The conductor's response was instantaneous. Cursing, he sprang up to the footboard and, using the butt of his open palm, began to beat the smaller man. The brutal work was unsatisfying, however, because the young man refused to fight back. Finally, as the victim's grip on the rail began to loosen, the conductor yielded to the half-hearted protests of the passengers who had come tumbling out of the coach to watch. Grudgingly, the conductor stepped over the driver's feet and took a third seat, occupied until then by a native Hottentot who had scrambled over the back of the seat to the safety of the luggage rack.

The young lawyer, after straightening himself, sat brooding as the stage rumbled on toward Johannesburg that day in 1893. The conductor pulled sullenly at his pipe, the passengers dozed, and the Hottentot man crouched over the luggage—none of them aware that the course of the history of two continents had suddenly changed. "I began to think of my duty," the young lawyer wrote later in his autobiography. "Should I fight for my rights or go back to India? . . . The hardship to which I was subject was . . . only a symptom of the deep disease of color prejudice. I should try, if possible to root out the disease."

There have been many eager fighters in the history of racial conflict, but only a few have used love as a weapon. The young man, at first only glimpsing its power, began by working with members of the colony of "coolie" laborers imported to South Africa from India, making them realize that to gain respect they must be self-improving, worthy of respect. During the course of twenty years he taught them, with increasing success, to achieve their goals through a program of nonviolence and passive disobedience to unjust and discriminatory laws. His own spiritual growth was slow. Years were to pass, for example, before he began to think of dark-skinned South Africans as having the same rights he claimed for his fellow Hindus—laborers and merchants alike. More years were to pass before the dapper young lawyer returned to his native India to become the spindly, bespectacled, rigorously self-disciplined leader and teacher whose memory is now universally revered. His philosophy matured bit by bit into what came in 1919 to be called the *satyagraha,* or "force of truth," or "truth-love"—a philosophy centered on the precept that outer or physical freedom comes only to those who know themselves to be spiritually free within. He often made mention of the fact that the maverick American philosopher, Henry David Thoreau, had been of invaluable assistance to him in the formation of basic philosophical and political positions.

In practice, the philosophy led to countless beatings, imprisonments, and even death for many disciples. His own life, which began in 1869, was ended by an assassin's bullet on January 30, 1948. But India's national freedom came, as he had said it would, when the people of that land sufficiently mastered the inner disciplines that made them free. The caste system that he abhorred started to break down, as he said it would, when the inherent dignity of all useful work began to be understood. The power of "superiors" over "inferiors" began to crumble that day when Mohandas Karamchand Gandhi, the Mahatma (or Great-Souled One), was beaten as he rode on the stagecoach to Johannesburg.

THE APOSTLE OF BEAUTY

John Muir and Conservation

There was no doubt in young John's mind that the years of back-breaking labor on the family farm had been given, as his father phrased it, "for the work of the Lord," since most of the farm profits went to support foreign missions. As an obedient son in the old-country tradition, he did not question his father's right to educate him by sitting with the Bible in one hand and a razor strop in the other while John committed long sections of the Bible to memory. But wouldn't it be possible, John speculated, to glorify God in other ways? They had come from Dunbar, Scotland, to the frontier farm in Wisconsin in 1849 when John was eleven years old. For almost ten years now the workday had extended from dawn until dark, with Bible lessons occupying the hours before bedtime. John, hungry for knowledge of other subjects, had constructed intricate wooden alarm clocks so he could be awakened before dawn and read books on mathematics and literature and texts in the field of knowledge that interested him most: natural science.

Professors at the University of Wisconsin had seen his prize-winning wooden clocks at the state fair and encouraged him to come to college, but his father protested angrily and forbade mention of the subject. Surely, thought John, the work of the Lord could be done in ways other than plowing, and the word of the Lord could be read in places other than the printed page. He had often stood at the edge of the unspoiled Wisconsin forests and marveled at the beauty in every tree and stream and living creature. The call to live in that world of God's nature was strong and could not be denied, and though heartsick at his father's refusal to bless him on his way—or even to touch his hand in a gesture of farewell—he left the farm and began his university studies. Four years later, after working his way through university, he undertook leisurely walking tours of Wisconsin, Illinois, and Indiana. In 1868 he first viewed the mighty Sierras of California, and for the twelve years following he traveled the length and breadth of the three-hundred-mile range, coming to know and love every kind of flower and animal, every variety of tree and shrub. It was here that he began to notice, and was quick to protest, the senseless stripping of the forests by lumber and mining interests, and he was shocked to learn that fires were purposely set and allowed to burn uncontrolled in order that more grazing land be made available. He watched, but not in silence, while ancient redwood trees crashed to earth, and joined his voice to the then tiny chorus of those who were beginning to fight against the plunder of America's natural beauty.

"People need beauty," he declared, "as well as bread. They need places to play in and pray in, where nature may heal and cheer and give strength to body and soul alike." In 1889 he campaigned successfully with Robert Underwood Johnson for the establishment of Yosemite National Park, and he worked at the same time for legislation that would establish a national park and forestry service. He had a leading part in establishing other national parks and served as an adviser to conservationist Theodore Roosevelt in setting aside millions of acres of forest reserves.

The name of John Muir (1838–1914) is, unfortunately, not well known to all Americans, but his work will continue to bless our land so long as men and women gaze reverently at the Grand Canyon's awesome and unmarred beauty, or stand appreciatively in the cathedral stillness of California's redwood groves. Muir's work, they will agree, was truly the work of the Lord.

THE MEANING OF MEMORIAL DAY

Mothers Loving and Forgiving

I t would be hard to ask the mother of a son who had been killed and buried on a battlefield to put flowers on the grave of an enemy soldier lying nearby. The point of this Memorial Day story is that nobody had to ask.

The Civil War was raging in 1863 when a bloody engagement took place at Columbus, Mississippi. Later in the spring of that same year, after the armies had moved away from the area, several Columbus women—some of whom had lost sons in the battle—made the short trip from the city to place flowers on the graves of their dead. The incident is nowhere described in full detail, but one may well imagine the terrible grief they shared on seeing the crudely marked graveyard. They could not have avoided the feeling that among the enemy dead lay the Union Army soldiers who had shot at, or perhaps even killed, their Confederate sons. One of the women, as she went about her task, realized that the mothers and loved ones of the dead Union soldiers were hundreds of miles away and unable to lay any token of remembrance on the graves. Without hesitation, she acted on their behalf by circling an "enemy" grave marker with a ring of blossoms. The others quickly followed suit, and they left the place that day knowing that in one simple act, however small, they had expressed feelings that are not a part of war—tenderness, love, and forgiveness.

The following year they returned to the grass-covered battle-field to repeat the memorial act, and on April 26, 1865, only two weeks after Robert E. Lee's surrender at Appomattox, a delegation of women traveled to Vicksburg, Mississippi, and decorated the graves of Union and Confederate soldiers there. Women in other parts of the South took up the practice annually in the spring, and within a few decades the idea had spread over the entire nation. In some sections of the country the term Decoration Day is still used; in other places it is called Memorial Day. Though originally intended to honor war dead, it has come to include, over time, all those whose lives are held in sacred remembrance. For many, the day is thought of grimly as a time of auto races and highway death statistics. Yet Americans should be proud to remember this: that on a particular day in a particular place, a certain grieving mother dropped a simple blossom on a patch of scarred earth. It was both a gesture of love and an act of forgiveness. That is the meaning of Memorial Day.

Another story of Memorial Day is set in Arlington National Cemetery soon after the Civil War. General James A. Garfield, who was later to become president, delivered a speech at the cemetery. With the War Department consenting, women of the area had decorated the graves of all of the Union soldiers, but, upon strict orders, had not placed flowers on the graves of three hundred Confederate soldiers who lay in a segregated section. After the crowd had left, according to the story, a great wind arose and blew most of the flowers on the Union graves over to the Confederate section.

There are a number of other stories about the beginnings of Memorial Day. Perhaps all of them, in their own way, convey truth.

"If I Come Back"

A Marine and the Bible

A lonely young Marine on a foreign battlefield, an anxious family waiting at home, a shared love of the Bible—these are the human factors that worked together in 1943 to bring about a unique, worldwide fellowship whose participants now number in the millions. A telephone call to the Philadelphia office of the American Bible Society started the spiritual chain reaction. A tearful mother called to say that she had received a letter from her son on Guadalcanal asking that the family join him in daily Bible reading. She read a portion of the letter and then hung up before the Bible Society member was able to get her name. She remains unknown to this day. But the notes hurriedly taken at the Bible Society as the young man's letter was read have become familiar to hosts of responsive souls:

> Out here, I have had time to think about the deeper things of the spiritual life. . . . Back home we went to church once in a while; but the fact is that the church and the Bible meant very little to us as a real power in our lives. I am writing you, Mom, to ask that you read with me a chapter from the New Testament each day. . . . This is my plan. Beginning about the middle of the month, you and Pop will read the first chapter of Mark, and I will read the first chapter way across the other side of the world. . . . I will feel that somehow we are united, sort of joining invisible hands; and I know that, if I come back, the church and the Bible will mean more to us than ever in our lives.

The Bible Society was quick to interpret this letter as a "request from an unknown Marine." His plan for day-by-day reading was publicized, and within a few weeks thousands joined in the prayerful endeavor.

Years later, the young man's wish continues to be fulfilled by an ever-increasing number of kindred spirits. The American Bible Society sponsors a daily Bible-reading fellowship, and the climax of the program each year is the worldwide reading of the Christmas story.

The homesick boy's letter contains a poignant phrase: "If I come back. . . ." We do not know whether he survived the dangers of World War II; we do not even know his name. But this may be said of him in surest tribute: He was obedient to God's command in the Bible—"Seek ye me, and ye shall live" (Amos 5:4a, KJV).

PART III

A Cloud of Witnesses

A SAINT IN AFRICA

Albert Schweitzer

When the deeply religious young doctor went to the jungles of Lambaréné, French Equatorial Africa, he was seeking obscurity, but he was rewarded with fame. He felt called to serve the tribespeople of a certain limited area, but his ministry has now been felt or appreciated in every nation on earth. He went there to help a relatively small number of people achieve health of body, but he assisted millions more in the quest for health of soul. He intended to give second place to his musical career, but now every organist and musical scholar in the world knows his name: Albert Schweitzer (1875–1965).

His story is without parallel in modern religious history. At the age of twenty-nine, happy and respected, he found himself at the peak of a career as concert organist and interpreter of Bach. Without warning he dropped it all to train for medicine and offer himself as a missionary doctor in Africa. Some called this decision a folly, a waste of talent. If so, it may be the most useful waste in history.

Why did he do it? "One brilliant summer morning," he explains, "there came to me as I awoke the thought that I must not accept this happiness as a matter of course, but must give something in return for it. Many a time already I had tried to settle what meaning lay hidden for me in the saying of Jesus: 'Whosoever would lose his life for my sake and the Gospel's shall save it.' Now the answer was found."

As the years of his African ministry passed by, Schweitzer become more and more respected as a New Testament scholar and theologian. The term "reverence for life," the principle of philosophy he expounded and tried to live by, became a familiar term; he was careful to emphasize the fact that in using the phrase he meant to include every living thing—*all* of life. Though his books are sometimes difficult reading for persons not trained in philosophy, he did not lose the ability to translate his basic ideas into plain, everyday language. At eighty-eight, the distinguished Lutheran and citizen of the world summed up much of his thought in these words:

> It is not enough merely to exist and say that you are doing your work well and earning enough to support your family. You must do something more. Every man has to seek in his own way to make his own self more noble and to realize his own true worth. You must give some time to your fellow man—something for those who have need of help, something for which you get no pay but the privilege of doing it. You don't live in a world all your own. Your brothers are here, too.

A certain ebony statue played an important part in the life of Schweitzer. It was a work of the sculptor Frédéric Auguste Bartholdi, and Schweitzer enjoyed thinking about its smooth, clean lines. He was fascinated by the heavy-browed, strong-jawed figure of the man it depicted. It seemed to express a basic dignity, a true nobility. History records that Albert Schweitzer, being inspired by Bartholdi's sculpture of a giant African, was moved to establish his hospital in Africa. As a medical missionary he ministered directly to the physical and spiritual needs of thousands, and—perhaps more important—by his example of intelligent compassion he was, for his time, a pioneer in smashing through the barriers of race and color, of culture and status. If and when peace comes among the nations and races, it will be because that same spirit of compassion flows to and from each of the now separate groups. The whole free world cherishes another statue by Bartholdi—the Statue of Liberty in New York harbor—but the people of Africa will always have a special love for the lesser-known black statue that brought to them a special kind of freeing spirit in a truly dedicated man.

THE HAS-BEEN

George Frideric Handel

G eorge eased his rheumatic frame into a green leather chair and stared without interest at the unopened envelope before him. Nothing, he thought, that the Rev. Charles Jennens, sender of the envelope, could say or write would change the facts: At fifty-six he was a musical has-been—the wells of creative ability, which in earlier years had made him a prolific composer, were dry. The once effusive critics and audiences knew it. Twisting uncomfortably in his chair on that unhappy afternoon in 1742, he looked out over the fog-laden London streets. How could a man be feted by cardinals and kings one day and be forgotten the next? How could a man have money to spare one day and not be able to hire singers and a hall on the next?

Absently, he tugged at the seal of the fat envelope and spread the contents on the table before him. There was a note from Jennens saying that the sheaves of papers attached were Bible verses compiled by a clerk named Pooley. Could they, inquired the clergyman, be set to music to tell the story of the coming of Christ? George started to read through the verses and suddenly caught his breath—they *were* music: "Comfort ye my people, saith your God. . . . Speak ye comfortably to Jerusalem . . . that her iniquity is pardoned. . . . I know that my Redeemer liveth. . . . Behold the Lamb of God. . . . Alleluia." With music swelling and bursting within him, George took up his pen and began to write. Oblivious now to physical pain, and feeling only the hand of God on his shoulder, he stayed in the room for twenty-four days, working day and night until the great oratorio *Messiah* was finished. As he was composing the now famous "Hallelujah Chorus," a servant entered the room to find him weeping with joy. "I thought I saw all Heaven before me," said Handel, "and the great God Himself!"

The new Christmas oratorio was received with great acclaim everywhere. An early audience, which included King George II of England, rose to its feet in a spontaneous act of astonishment and respect during the singing of the powerful "Hallelujah Chorus," starting a custom practiced to this day. George Frideric Handel (1685–1759), who later set many sections of the Bible to music, was surprised and pleased to find he cared less and less for honors now, for he had found serenity in his work.

LADIES AND GENTLEMEN, OUR NATIONAL ANTHEM

Francis Scott Key

S poken prayer sometimes can be made through clenched teeth, supplicating hands may be tightly formed into hard fists, and the heart from which the prayers flow can be filled with desperate anxiety. So it was with young Francis in the deep night of September 13, 1814, as he waited aboard a truce ship and stared out through the misted darkness toward Maryland's Fort McHenry. His long prayer watch had begun in the early evening of that day, as he and other American truce party members who had gone to negotiate the release of a prisoner waited aboard their small sloop, which lay at anchor, under British guard, on Chesapeake Bay near the mouth of the Patapsco River. In the quick-falling darkness he had caught a last glimpse of the American flag that flew over the fort, and as the bombs flew—hundreds upon hundreds in the direction of the fragile banner—he wondered if the great hopes and dreams that it symbolized would vanish with the dawn.

Four weeks earlier soldiers from the attacking British fleet had marched into Washington, D.C., where they set fire to the Capitol, the White House, and many other buildings. Now, with the bombardment of Fort McHenry, Baltimore's key defense point, the whole of the Eastern seaboard lay in peril. During the night British troops had landed for a flank attack, and small ships carrying rockets had moved to within close range of the important target. It was shortly after 1 A.M. on the morning of September 14 when the bombardment abruptly stopped. The black hours that followed were illuminated only by occasional flares that revealed the shadowy hulks of the warships. The hour of dawn approached, the tension grew, and the Americans stood in silence as the first gray bars of morning appeared on the horizon. Suddenly the silence was broken by shouts and cheers: The flag was still there. The British, having tested the defenses and found them sure, had taken their troops back aboard and headed toward another objective. Francis Scott Key reached inside his waistcoat, searching for something to write on. He pulled out an envelope and on it began to scribble the lines of the poem that has since become our national anthem.

As the sloop made its way to Baltimore, Key continued his work and later in a hotel room finished it. The poem was printed in handbill form by the *Baltimore Patriot* the next day, and in the following weeks it quickly became known and admired in every section of the country. The music to which the poem eventually was set is an old English marching tune of uncertain authorship, and the less sophisticated but very enthusiastic patriots of that day did not complain about it being "unsingable." Francis Scott Key (1779–1843), the son of a Revolutionary War officer, wrote only a few other poems. One of these, "Lord, With Glowing Heart I Praise Thee," is preserved in the 1982 Episcopal Hymnal. He was a lawyer and served as U.S. district attorney for three terms. He spent much of his time visiting the sick, and worked as a lay reader and Sunday school teacher in the Episcopal church. He was a prayerful man and a patriot, as the following verses will forever attest:

> Oh! say, can you see, by the dawn's early light,
> What so proudly we hailed at the twilight's last gleaming?
> Whose broad stripes and bright stars, thro' the perilous fight,
> O'er the ramparts we watched were so gallantly streaming?
> And the rockets' red glare, the bombs bursting in air,
> Gave proof thro' the night that our flag was still there.
> Oh! say, does the star-spangled banner yet wave
> O'er the land of the free and the home of the brave?

HOUSTON'S GREATEST VICTORY

Sam Houston

S am squirmed uneasily in his seat in the Baptist church in Washington and listened with what was almost contempt as the preacher spoke of the battles men must wage to gain control of their own souls. Sam, who had come to church that day in 1854 to please his wife, was the last person on earth who needed to be told about battles of any kind. With 743 raw troops he had routed 1,600 veteran Mexican soldiers at the battle of San Jacinto, and he had captured their general, Santa Anna, the next day. Sam was tough. He had fought with the Indians and against them. He had fought corruption in federal Indian agencies. He had successfully defended his own honor in the midst of accusations of dishonesty. He could out-fight, out-cuss and out-drink anybody his own size or double.

The preacher, he conceded after a while, was no slouch at laying it on the line. "Better is he who rules his spirit than he who takes a city," the speaker declared, and as he listened Sam realized that the man was proving the point. It was then that Senator Sam Houston (1793–1863), colorful and courageous military and political leader, ceased to hear what the preacher was saying. Instead, the man after whom a great city was to be named was deep in his own thoughts—his spirit stilled by the realization that this was his moment for a face-to-face encounter with the Prince of Peace. It was true, he mused, that he had won every battle except the one against his own intemperate habits and speech. As the minutes passed, he was surprised to find that he felt no sense of shame or despair in facing up to these weaknesses. To the contrary, he felt a calm assurance that with the help of God he could win this battle of soul as well. And he did.

Upon the adjournment of Congress, Houston returned imme-diately to Texas and was baptized by the Rev. Dr. Rufus C. Burleson in the city of Independence. With the passing of years he became an ever stronger advocate of Christianity and interested himself in the distribution of religious literature and in Baptist missionary work among the Indians. He became a forceful, example-setting champion of temperance and found time as well to serve as a trustee of Baylor University. In 1859 he was elected governor of Texas and was deposed from his office in 1861 when he refused to swear allegiance to the Confederacy. He died two years later without having seen his political stand vindicated, but he died a man confident of the eternal victory he had won in the battle for his soul.

THE INTRUDER

Robert E. Lee

The distinguished group of Virginia ladies and gentlemen who had assembled for worship at Richmond's most fashionable church that Sunday shortly after the close of the Civil War would never have thought of committing an act of physical violence within the sacred confines of the building, but reddening necks above the white starched collars showed that their rising anger might very well bring about that unhappy circumstance. All eyes were focused on the source of their anger, an African American man who, having entered the church just after the beginning of the service, was now walking slowly, and alone, toward the altar rail as it came time for the people to receive Communion. The vested celebrant stood dumbfounded and motionless, chalice in hand, as the intruder moved nearer. The women in the congregation were speechless, too stunned even to whisper, and it seemed that at any moment the dreadful, ominous silence would burst.

What they saw approaching the altar was not only a man breaking a long-standing tradition; he was a living symbol of their lost cause, a reason for the death of husbands and sons and fathers who had only a short time before worshiped with them at this very altar. He was the reason, they thought, for their loss of land and property; he was the reason for the breaking down of a genteel and courtly way of life. Minutes earlier they had listened while the Episcopal priest recited the familiar invitation to Communion: "Ye who do truly and earnestly repent you of your sins, and are in love and charity with your neighbors, and intend to lead a new life . . . ." They had joined in the General Confession, admitting their "manifold sins and wickedness." They had prayed for forgiveness of all that was past, and they had received the assurance of God's pardon. Now, they felt, the ancient beauty of the service was being marred, their prayers were being mocked, the privacy of their worship was being invaded. They felt they were watching a monstrous travesty in the making—and the men made ready to move.

Just at that moment they became aware of another person in the aisle moving up behind the African American man. The silence was broken by murmurs of surprise as they recognized their most distinguished layman—a loyal and earnest churchman who, as chance would have it, had become a living symbol of all that was good and noble in the South. They watched in what suddenly became respectful quiet as the two men knelt together at the Communion rail. With the evil tension gone, members of the congregation were able to try to find within themselves the right spirit of worship, and as they did several others were moved to join the two at the Communion rail.

The dream of integrated worship in the South was not, unfortunately, realized that day, but a creative start, however small, was made. Sometime, in a world that is yet to be, when this problem is only a painful memory, people will look back and thank the courageous unknown African American man and General Robert E. Lee (1807–1870), the distinguished layman who acted so wisely and gracefully that day in Richmond, for the part they played as individuals in bringing peace between the races.

THE CONTRIBUTION
OF A FREED SLAVE

Amos Fortune

Writers of fiction have given us many stories of the search for the Holy Grail, the legendary Communion cup said to have been used by Jesus at the Last Supper. The precious vessel has become a symbol of humanity's unity with God. Some searchers, like the knights of King Arthur's court, have sought it through deeds of valor. Amos Fortune of Jaffrey, New Hampshire, had a simpler solution: He made possible the purchase of one that would serve the purpose nicely for plain, hard cash. He was an African American man, a former slave who had purchased his freedom and gone to work as a tanner in the little town of Jaffrey. He was good at his trade and, because of his obvious excellence of character, he enjoyed a certain degree of respect. But friendship offered strictly within the limits of what people thought was his "proper place" was sometimes almost worse than no friendship at all. Many times, in the course of what would start out to be pleasant chats, he had the frustrating and sometimes heartbreaking feeling that he had suddenly come up against a cold, invisible wall. He was near and yet very far from real friendship.

Amos loved to go to church, and his desire for fellowship was honored—up to a point. He was permitted to attend if he sat in a segregated gallery, but he was not allowed to participate in the Communion service. It was while sitting in the gallery that Amos Fortune came to some important conclusions. He resolved that prejudice against him would not destroy his own desire for truly Christian fellowship or turn it into an ugly spirit of hatred and revenge. The prayer of Jesus that all people might be one should be honored, he thought, and the teaching of the Sermon on the

Mount that people should bless and pray for those who spitefully used them must be obeyed at whatever cost.

As he looked down at the worshiping congregation he noticed that the Communion vessels were of quite an ordinary type, and the thought occurred to him that only the finest and most beautiful things should be used in this holiest of acts. He knew that some day, in the providence of God, there would be one Lord, one altar, one cup, and one great fellowship of compassionate goodwill and love. Amos Fortune never tasted of that cup. He lived quietly for many years, managing to get along on the crumbs of friendship that, in a manner of speaking, fell from the tables of those who had plenty to spare.

When he died in 1801 (at about 91 years of age, so he thought—born a slave, he did not know his date or place of birth), the townspeople were surprised to discover that he had willed a substantial part of his modest estate to the town school where his daughter had suffered through years of harassment and ridicule. Another gift, to be used for the purchase of a Communion set—a set fine enough to reflect the beauty of the moment when people of every nation and race would worship in true communion—he left to the Congregational church he had attended.

Now, many decades later, a distinguished lecture series has been established in his memory. But more important, the silver chalice he gave becomes, for moments at least, the Holy Grail as people of different races share it, and find in sharing their unity with God.

THE EXAMINATION

Booker T. Washington

The anxious and busy youth, a freed slave, went over the schoolroom again and again—dusting and praying, praying and sweeping—glancing frequently at the doorway through which the teacher would come. She had told him to clean the room while he waited for a decision by Hampton Institute officials on his application for admission as a student, and he had just finished his third inch-by-inch cleaning of the room.

There had been much waiting that afternoon in 1872. Several hours had passed since he arrived at the school, dusty and tired after the five-hundred-mile journey by foot, wagon, and railroad freight car. He knew that without a bath or change of clothes he had not made a very favorable impression, and he sickened at the thought of being turned away. Then, as if he had willed it, the door opened and the teacher appeared. Flourishing her dainty white handkerchief, she walked around the room brushing the cloth over the woodwork and benches. After several minutes she held up the unsoiled handkerchief and smiled—and at that moment Booker T. Washington became a student and a janitor at the institute.

The rustic living quarters assigned to him were palatial compared with the dirt-floored, windowless slave cabin he had left, and the simple meals at the school were kingly beside the boiled corn that was the steady diet of slaves and livestock in the place from which he had come. School officials, pleased from the first with his work, were astounded at his learning ability, and it soon became apparent that he had a great future in education. At twenty-five, he was chosen to establish and head a school at Tuskegee, Alabama, for the training of African Americans in the trades and professions. Beginning with forty students housed in a rickety shack, the school grew rapidly until, at the time of his death in 1915, there were more than a hundred buildings, two hundred teachers, fifteen hundred students, and endowments and other properties valued in excess of two million dollars.

Booker Taliaferro Washington (1856–1915), saw as his special task the healing of the breach between the races, and he devoted his life energetically and prayerfully to that end. "There is no defense or security for any of us," he said, "except in the highest intelligence and development of all." President Theodore Roosevelt called upon him often for counsel and honored him many times with the declaration that the educator perfectly fulfilled the biblical truth stated in Micah 6:8: "What does the Lord require of you but to do justice, and to love kindness, and to walk humbly with your God?"

Washington often referred to the room-dusting incident as the most important examination he ever passed, and it is certainly true that much of modern history hung in the balance that day. People of all races might well remember that perhaps some of our most severe racial "examinations" or tests are yet to come—and we will all have to lean heavily on the advice of Micah in order to pass.

THE RANSOMED SLAVE BABY

George Washington Carver

The sick slave baby wasn't worth much, but the mother would bring a good price, so the plundering band, one of many that plagued the South during the Civil War, carried them away. As predicted, the mother was sold without difficulty, but the infant, wracked with whooping cough, was a problem. The marauders could scarcely believe their good luck when a ransom-paying emissary from the Newton County, Missouri, plantation where they had stolen the slave woman and her baby finally caught up with them after days of patient trailing. His offer of a three-hundred-dollar racehorse in exchange for the baby was accepted quickly, and the kidnappers went on their way, rejoicing. Close friends of the plantation owner, a thrifty German named Moses, knew that his wife loved the child as her own.

The boy never became strong enough to work in the fields, so he was assigned to the kitchen. He loved flowers and plants and spent endless hours studying and cultivating them. A nervous stammer led him away from company with others. When he was ten years old, George left the plantation and for seven years worked his way through schools where he could gain admission. Finally he was accepted at the college at Indianola, Iowa. His incredible talent for plant science began to blossom, and he showed a fine ability in music and art as well. After graduation, he felt called to join Booker T. Washington's famed school at Tuskegee, Alabama.

He thought of his work as a kind of ministry. His research on cotton and soil was of inestimable benefit to farmers. When the supply of aniline dyes from Germany was cut off during World War I, he perfected vegetable dyes as substitutes. He discovered more than 250 medicinal properties of plants. His research on the lowly peanut yielded more than 300 products, including soap, ink, face cream, paints, flavors, axle grease, and shampoos. Soon he was acknowledged as the nation's foremost agricultural scientist.

He was never impressed by money or signs of wealth. His salary at Tuskegee was $1,500 a year, and very often he misplaced or forgot to cash his paycheck. The offer of $175,000 a year by Thomas Edison could not budge him from Tuskegee, nor could Henry Ford offer enough money to take him away. A valuable diamond in a ring given to him by a friend was taken out of its setting and placed in a case of humble mineral specimens.

The sick slave baby, ransomed by love, was George Washington Carver (1864?–1943). He received his last name from the man who owned him when he was born and his first two names "because of his honesty." His full name has its own special meaning in America now: greatness.

DE PROFUNDIS . . .

Henry Lyte

The quiet surface of Brixham harbor, shimmering gold only moments before, was darkening now as the autumn sun dipped below the horizon, and the masts and spars of the trawling vessels lying peacefully at anchor began to form shadowy crosses against the twilight sky. Looking down from the parsonage garden, the Rev. Henry Lyte could see symbolized in all these things the tragic story of his life. The twenty-four years he had spent as the Anglican parson of Brixham, England, had seemed for the most part bright and golden indeed, but now, during the final days of his ministry, dark clouds of unprovoked anger and senseless dissension had appeared. It was the eventide of his life, he knew, and with seriously failing health there would be no strength for the patching up of difficulties—no fresh start. The kind of life he had tried to live and to give the villagers had been crucified by their hatred; it was as if he had never worked and lived and prayed among them at all.

The dejected pastor, barely able to carry the double burden of sickness and defeat, walked slowly toward the house and, without disturbing the other members of his family, slipped quietly into his study. There on the desk lay his well-thumbed Bible, open at the twenty-fourth chapter of Luke's Gospel. He placed his forefinger on the margin of the twenty-ninth verse and read in a whisper the familiar plea made by the disciples to Jesus: "Abide with us; for it is toward evening, and the day is far spent" (KJV). The day was far spent, to be sure. There might be time, his doctor had said, for a leisurely vacation rest in Italy, but beyond that Henry had no right to hope. What is left, he pondered, after hope is gone, after friends and health and even life is gone? One thing was left, he knew, just one—God. God was the ultimate necessity, and, in holy writ, God had promised to abide.

Henry Francis Lyte, suddenly strengthened by these thoughts, reached into a side drawer of the desk and drew out a sheet of paper on which he had written a few sketchy notes for a poem he had been composing, and within minutes the poem, "Abide with Me," was completed. Lyte sailed for Italy the next day but managed to travel only as far as Nice, France, where he died. Some years later the poem was discovered among his papers and was set to music by William H. Monk in 1874. Other poems subsequently discovered include "Praise, My Soul, the King of Heaven" and "Jesus, I My Cross Have Taken." They are now among the favorites of millions.

But "Abide with Me," the song born in adversity, has become the gold of the church and has glorified the cross its author bore.

> Abide with me: Fast falls the eventide;
> The darkness deepens; Lord, with me abide!
> When other helpers fail, and comforts flee,
> Help of the helpless, O abide with me.
> . . . .
> Hold Thou Thy cross before my closing eyes;
> Shine through the gloom and point me to the skies
> Heaven's morning breaks, and earth's vain shadows flee;
> In life, in death, O Lord, abide with me.
> —Henry Francis Lyte (1793–1847)

"JUST AS I AM"

Charlotte Elliott

Resentment against the visiting clergyman's pious inquiry into the state of her religious conditions burned in Charlotte's mind, and she lost no time in putting him in his place. The fact that she, at thirty-two, had become a bedfast invalid and would remain so for life did not mean that she was bereft of all mental powers. Invalid or not, she declared, she had a right to privacy and she certainly did not want the pity of an oversolicitous clergyman. After all, she had two brothers in the ministry who would give her spiritual guidance if, and only if, she asked them. Her anger subsided only slightly when her visitor, the Rev. Caesar Malan, "apologized" by saying he was sorry to learn of her feelings but would continue to pray that she would come to love and serve Christ.

After he had gone, she suffered some vague sense of regret for the way she had acted. The man had meant well, she felt, but he simply could not begin to understand the bitter caricature of life that an invalid endures. As to her deep personal need for divine companionship, who could need it more? And who on earth had less hope of finding it? When he visited her the following week her mood was different, but equally unhappy. The demon of self-sufficiency was gone, but in its place were seven demons of hopelessness, and she confessed, "I do not know how to find Christ—I want you to help me." Malan's answer was brief: "Come to him just as you are."

At first the sentence had little meaning for Charlotte Elliott—it was too brief and too simple—but after days of thought and prayer she found it to be the key that opened the door to the first real inner peace she had ever known. The phrase was never far from her conscious mind in the days that followed, and she found herself enshrining it in a simple poem. Evangelist Dwight L. Moody later declared that the poem written by the woman who was destined to live creatively for half a century as an almost helpless invalid has, in its hymn form, "done the most good, to the greatest number, and has touched more lives helpfully than any other hymn." However that may be, it is certain that Charlotte Elliott's transforming experience will bless people for generations to come. This is her poem:

> Just as I am, without one plea
> But that Thy blood was shed for me,
> And that Thou biddest me come to Thee,
> O Lamb of God, I come, I come.
>
> . . . .
>
> Just as I am, Thou wilt receive,
> Wilt welcome, pardon, cleanse, relieve;
> Because Thy promise I believe,
> O Lamb of God, I come, I come.
>   —Charlotte Elliott (1789–1871)

THE SLENDER THREAD

Toyohiko Kagawa

The young man's life was ebbing quietly away as the weakening rays of the late afternoon sun settled over Japan. Beneath the haze of tuberculosis fever he lay praying, waiting for the final breath. The suffering twenty-year-old Toyohiko Kagawa, gifted son of a noted Japanese politician and his concubine, had first seen the light of day on July 12, 1888, and had been raised by his stepmother and grandmother in an atmosphere of hatred and resentment. His lonely search for faith had led him to a thoughtful rejection of Buddhism and Confucianism. He had turned at seventeen to the Christian faith, where he felt that new vistas of the soul opened before him. "O God, make me like Christ," he had cried as he read the Sermon on the Mount. In the deepening twilight he sighed a prayer to God that the slender thread of life might hold, that he might live to serve the One he called Lord. As he prayed, the veil of fever was lifted—the shadow of death was gone.

The disease was to persist for many years, but his pledge was translated immediately into action in the slums of Kobe, where for fourteen years he was to be found working from early morning until late at night preaching, counseling, planning, writing, and battling poverty. He was deeply involved in farm and labor problems and became a living symbol of social welfare and reform. His life crested in crisis again and again. A dagger once poised threateningly over his head clattered to the pavement as the assailant who held it heard the words from Toyohiko's lips: "Father, forgive. . . ." His sight was severely damaged by disease and his front teeth were broken off by a drunken bully, but the sight of his frail body was enough to halt a surging mob of thirty-five thousand angry strikers once bent on destroying the shipyards at Kobe. Placing himself on a narrow bridge over which the mob would have to pass to reach the shipyard, he stood, praying that violence would cease. The near-hysterical workers, as they approached him, came face to face with their conscience, then turned away in silence and settled the dispute by the peaceful means he had proposed earlier on their behalf. "Where love is at work," he said, "there is God."

Toyohiko Kagawa (1888–1960) was at once a symbol and a force. Though imprisoned for a time during World War II for his pacifist views, he never ceased to direct his limitless energy in the service of the reality he knew as the God of love and peace. The scholarly talents he developed at the Presbyterian College in Tokyo yielded more than 150 books on subjects ranging from soil science to sermons. Evangelist, teacher, poet, philosopher, scientist, saint—his work will go on because three prayers were answered: "Father, forgive . . . ," "God, let me live to serve," and "O God, make me like Christ."

THE WITNESS OF SUFFERING

Katherine Mansfield

John Murry, a confirmed agnostic, looked at the slip of paper on which his young wife's last prayer had been written: "Lord, make me crystal clear for Thy light to shine through." There was a luminous, hard-to-describe kind of quality in the prayer, he felt, a quality that had permeated her whole personality. After searching his mind for a word that would accurately describe its meaning he concluded, almost reluctantly, that there was only one term that would really apply: resurrection. Katherine Murry, better remembered by her pen name, Katherine Mansfield, was a gifted writer who left a large treasure of short stories and poems (and a small packet of deliciously scandalous personal escapades) before her death from tuberculosis at the age of thirty-four (1888–1923). Her struggle with the disease extended over many years, and no fictional hero born in her imagination ever faced life with such courage and determination. As death finally drew near, she discovered an important stepping-stone between suffering and death: acceptance, acceptance without defeat.

Her private journal tells the story:

I should like this to be accepted as my confession. There is no limit to human suffering. When one thinks, "Now I have touched the bottom of the sea—now I can go no deeper," one does go deeper. But I do not want to die without leaving a record of my belief that suffering can be overcome. For I do believe it. What must one do? Do not resist. Take it. Be overwhelmed. Accept it fully. Make it a part of life. Everything in life that we really accept undergoes a change. So suffering in life that we really accept undergoes a change. . . .

Suffering, as a part of her life, was thus consecrated, offered to God for blessing, and its power to damage her soul was gone. Something died: fear. Something was born: acceptance in the spirit of love.

While reading these lines, Murry suddenly became faced with his own problem of acceptance. He had resisted faith in the same manner that she had at first resisted pain. But why resist, he thought—why not accept it fully and make it a part of life? Something died that day in John Murry: doubt. Something was born: a loving faith.

Murry is remembered not as the dull and anonymous husband of a famous writer, but as a distinguished priest of the Church of England, a vocation for which he prepared himself after her death. He saw in her life a ray of glory "shining through" from another, ancient triumph of love over the forces of suffering and sin. As he had shared in her life and victory, so, he said, he had indeed shared in Christ's.

THE COMMENCEMENT PRAYER

Mary McLeod Bethune

It was a June night in South Carolina. The air drifting through the glassless windows of the rickety two-room shack was heavy and sweet. The silence was broken now and again by the distant cry of a night-prowling animal and by the occasional sounds of restless stirring by one of the twenty members of the Bethune family who were taking their rest in the crowded rooms. Mary, sleepless, the seventeenth child of freed slave parents, rose quietly from her place on the floor and tiptoed to the window where she knelt to look out and share her gratitude with God in prayer. The exciting news had come today that she would be allowed to attend the Presbyterian-founded Scotia Seminary at Concord, North Carolina, and this, the teenaged girl thought, was more than enough reward for the effort she had made these last six years in walking five miles each day to study hard at the mission school. There had been family prayers earlier in the day—indeed, the Bethune family assembled every morning and every evening for prayer—but this graduation night was special and her heart overflowed with prayers of thanksgiving. What could the young girl give? Only one thing, she knew—herself.

The year was 1890, and Mary's gift of herself to God that night led first to demanding but successful study at Scotia Seminary, then to further work at the Moody Bible Institute in Chicago, and then to a teaching career at Haines Institute in Augusta, Georgia. In 1904, with incredible energy and limitless determination but with almost no equipment or money, she started a school for girls at Daytona Beach, Florida. The venture was blessed, and in 1922 her school was made coeducational as it joined with the Cookman School for Boys. Growing recognition of her splendid work led to her appointment by President Franklin D. Roosevelt in the difficult Depression year of 1934 as head of the work among African American people under the National Youth Administration. In World War II she served as a special assistant to the Secretary of War in selecting candidates for the Women's Army Corps officer school. In 1945, at the age of seventy, she served with the United States delegation in the founding of the United Nations in San Francisco, her special area of interest being racial affairs. She was showered with honorary university degrees and government awards, including the Thomas Jefferson Medal. She was honored by the National Association for the Advancement of Colored People by being made its vice-president, and in 1954 she was awarded the title "Mother of the Century" by the Dorie Miller Foundation. She was the beloved friend and patron of James Mercer Langston Hughes, the premier African American poet.

At commencement time in any year, all of us will have reason to be thankful for the prayer-blessed talents of Mary McLeod Bethune (1875–1955), and thoughtful people the world over will be grateful for the joyfully consecrated gift of her life.

THE SECOND MIRACLE

Alexis Carrel

The pale morning light showing now in the east brought no
illumination to the spirit of the young physician who sat
confused and exhausted beside the window of his hotel
room. The place was Lourdes, the healing mecca of France, and
the time was a summer dawn in 1903. The long hours of the night
had been spent in aimless walking along the quiet streets of the
famed healing center while he struggled to face the fact that he
had in truth witnessed a miracle in the dramatic recovery of a new
acquaintance, a young woman named Marie. His once pleasant
and comfortable skepticism was shattered, gone, and in its place
was—nothing!

In the attempt to introduce some scientific order into his
jumbled thoughts, he reviewed the remarkable series of recent
events. In quest of a reasonable scientific answer for the many
reported miracles at Lourdes he had decided to go there himself,
camera in hand. On the train to Lourdes he had examined young
Marie (Ferrand) Bailly and found her to be suffering terribly from
a terminal case of tubercular peritonitis. The symptoms were
unmistakable, obvious, and undeniable. After the passage of several days at the shrine, during which she received no medication or
surgical treatment, he had examined her again and found her to be
completely cured—with only shrunken scars to testify to the
former presence of the disease. Something that could not possibly
happen had happened, and the meaning, he knew, lay hidden in
God. Kneeling now, he opened himself in prayer. "Let me believe
implicitly, passionately . . . ," he prayed. "Give me the gift of
certitude of belief." For long minutes he knelt there, increasingly
unaware of time or place or state of mind, and when at length he

arose he found himself in a bright and clear new life. A second miracle had taken place—the gift of faith was his!

Dr. Alexis Carrel (1873–1944) in later life came to be recognized as one of the best physiological surgeons of the century. His natural skill and fitness as a surgeon (for exercise he would make as many as five hundred stitches along the edge of a cigarette paper) led him to develop a vastly improved method of suturing blood vessels, making possible safer blood transfusions. He developed a technique for transplanting entire blood vessels. He received the Nobel Prize for this work; on another occasion he was awarded the Nordhoff-Jung Medal for cancer research. With Henry Dakin, he developed an antiseptic solution that saved many lives and prevented countless amputations during World War I. For thirty-three years he was a research professor at the Rockefeller Institute and engaged in pioneer research with Charles A. Lindbergh on a mechanical heart.

A baptized Roman Catholic, he at one time—before Lourdes—"outgrew" his faith, but after his experience there and with the help of his close friend and pastor, the French Abbé of Boquen, he eventually "grew back in" more firmly than before. With all his scientific ability, he declared repeatedly that prayer is the most powerful force in the world. His popular essay, "Prayer Is Power," which appeared in *Reader's Digest* in 1940, is still read by millions in its reprint form; perhaps this essay will turn out to be his most important legacy. The study of humanity, he said, is a pathway to God—but the ultimate pathway is prayer.

THE SPENDTHRIFT PRIEST

Father Dominique Georges Pire

The white-clad Dominican priest, a studious Belgian pro-
fessor-pastor, had no way of knowing that the speech he
was listening to with such keen interest that night in 1949
would eventually put into—and take out of—his pocket more than
half a million dollars from such curiously varied sources as a
Masonic lodge, a Catholic bishop, a poverty-stricken French
seamstress, and the Nobel Peace Prize Fund. The speaker, a
visiting American supervisor of a displaced-persons camp in Aus-
tria, was telling Father Dominique Georges Pire and his group of
young Belgian students about the almost unbearable circum-
stances in which many pathetic survivors of the recent war were
still living.

When the speech ended, several of the deeply concerned young
people rose to ask if they could assist the refugees in some way.
The American, after suggesting that they could help by writing
letters to the survivors, gave them a list of forty-seven names.
Father Pire was delighted at the opportunity for person-to-person
contact with these uprooted families and individuals who were
without home or job or country. As chaplain and intelligence
officer in the Belgian resistance movement, he had seen the
sorrows of world strife firsthand, and he was grateful now to be
able to direct his ministry in this positive and specific way toward
healing the wounds of war. Within a matter of hours he had
written to all the names on the list. Soon after, he went on a
personal tour of the camp areas, and almost before he realized
what was happening he found that he was devoting the whole of
his time and talent to relief work.

His patient interest in individual refugees struck a deep chord of response in his friends and acquaintances, and more than a thousand persons joined him in sending letters, packages, gifts, and money. The movement grew until at one time there were sixteen thousand men and women from more than two dozen countries sending some one hundred thousand letters each year. The half-million dollars mentioned earlier meant homes for the aged, scholarships for the young, villages for the homeless, and food for the hungry. It meant medicine, clothing, and travel expenses to resettlement areas for hundreds of families. But it meant something much more important: compassionate care that can never be measured in terms of dollars.

Father Pire's successful appeal to what he called "the heart of Europe" overcame every kind of national, racial, cultural, and religious barrier. On the wall of his modest office in the Belgian city of Huy were photographs of Albert Schweitzer, a Protestant, and Mohandas Gandhi, a Hindu—personal friends, and only two of the hundreds of close friendships he maintained with individuals of almost every religious persuasion. In 1958 the tall, sturdy Belgian, at forty-eight, became the first Roman Catholic priest in history to receive the Nobel Peace Prize, and he immediately put the forty-one thousand dollars of prize money to work for his refugee friends.

Many governments, religious organizations, and interested individuals worked together in the mammoth effort to minister to the needs of the refugees after World War II. When the final chapter on this tragic part of world history is closed, the credit for whatever good that has been done will be shared by many, but there will always be a particular spot in "the heart of Europe," and of the world, for Dominique Georges Pire (1910–1969)— God's cheerful spendthrift of money and love—who was able to see not problems but people, and who dedicated himself to helping them one by one.

THE PAGAN SON

Lin Yutang

It is not unheard of for the children of clergymen to break away from the faith in which they have been nurtured, but it is a rare thing indeed when one of them becomes world famous by writing a book in defense of paganism. Lin Yutang, the son of a Presbyterian minister in China's Paoa Valley, was raised in a home where Christianity was intelligently taught and lovingly practiced. Upon reaching young manhood he began to study for the ministry, but intellectual difficulties over what he said was "theological hocus-pocus" caused him to drop Christianity entirely.

His awakening appreciation of ancient Chinese culture and the desire to retain some form of belief in God led him to embrace Confucianism, and enthusiasm for this religion expressed itself years later in the writing of a book that became a worldwide best seller, *The Importance of Living.* In this book he defended what he called paganism and explained that the excellent Confucian ideal of human dignity was completely satisfying. An intelligent person, he felt, could place his faith in the idea that people, through their own reason and power, could make a better world.

This humanistic philosophy ultimately disappointed him. Lin Yutang's long study of history—both in the East and West—convinced him that when people reject the idea that there is a higher power outside themselves, they cease to grow godward and fall into a materialistic outlook on life. The high moral teaching of Confucius was impressive, yet, in Lin's words, "It was not enough . . . because man on his own had so often and disastrously shown he was not that good." Moreover, he was able over the years to see the corrosive and destructive effects of the "humans are God" philoso-

111

phy as it was espoused by the Communists who came into control of China.

By 1957, thirty years after Lin left Christianity, the wheel completed its turn. The man whose name had by that time become associated with all that is beautiful and relevant in Chinese wisdom literature turned once more to the study of the Bible. Freed from what he called the dogmatist's blinders, he was able, so he said, to see for the first time the majestically emerging revelation of God in Christ. His own study, together with the brilliant preaching of David Read at the Madison Avenue Presbyterian Church in New York City (where he had gone to live), resulted in Lin's decision to return to Christianity. This news spread quickly through Asia, and the effect of his decision among intellectuals there, though hard to evaluate, was of undoubted significance.

The famous Chinese scholar and writer (1895–1976) described the teachings of Christ as "soul charging and of incomparable beauty."

"That Person and that Gospel I have found sufficient," he says. "Nothing less than that Person and Gospel can be sufficient for the world."

THE "MOSES" WHO LED AFRICAN AMERICANS INTO BASEBALL

Jackie Robinson

T he older man, a prominent baseball figure, suddenly changed his matter-of-fact, businesslike expression and turned on the young African American athlete. "A nigger is a nigger," he bellowed, "and that's all he'll ever be!" The young man, stiff with hurt and surprise, clenched and unclenched his fists threateningly, but the older man moved closer and kicked him hard on the shins in contempt. Then it was over. The older man—the baseball-team owner—stepped back, and the two men studied each other in silence.

The younger man spoke: "Why do you have to say these things to me, Mr. Rickey?" Branch Rickey, owner of the Brooklyn Dodgers and distinguished leader in the world of baseball, dropped the false pose he had taken, smiled, and placed his hand gently on the young man's shoulder.

Moments earlier they had been discussing the possibility of a career in big-time baseball for the young African American man, Jackie Robinson. The year was 1945, and Negroes (as African Americans were then called) were barred by race from the major leagues. Rickey had heard of Jackie Robinson's amazing college football and baseball achievements and had learned also that his sincere religious beliefs had shown themselves in his excellence of character and wholesomeness of habit. Rickey had warned Robinson that he would have to have two things to get into the big leagues: the ability to play the game with the best, and the ability to stand the heat of what would be massive resentment toward the first African American player in major-league baseball. In testing Jackie's patience in the latter, Rickey had tried to demonstrate, through pretended anger, something of the hate Robinson would meet. "Do you think," said the manager, referring to his dramatic and realistic portrayal of a bigot, "that you can get through this kind of thing?"

"I can," replied Robinson softly, "if I pray."

Rickey's prediction of trouble ahead could not have been more accurate. There were cancelled games, boos in the stadium, slashing steel spikes on the playing field, insult after insult, and boring, uncomfortable hours in fleabag hotels where he was forced to stay, segregated from his teammates. For many months the pain of loneliness was more bitter than all the rest. Teammates shut him out of their close fellowship and refused even to give him the traditional handshake and cheer when crossing the plate after a home run. But Jackie stuck it out. Both he and Rickey were later honored by induction into baseball's Hall of Fame.

Anyone who has followed the game during the nearly five decades since Jackie's breakthrough knows that his magnificent playing ability won him the title "Rookie of the Year" in 1947, and fans became aware of the prayer-born patience that made him one of the great men of the game. No one should have to qualify for sainthood in order to play baseball, but Jackie Robinson humbled himself—lowered himself, if you will. He lowered himself the way people do when they crouch to press their shoulder against a heavy obstacle. The obstacle in this case was prejudice. Thanks to Jackie Robinson (1919–1972), who opened the game—and to other fine and courageous players among all minority groups—the obstacle is steadily moving away.

THE ROAD NOT TAKEN

Robert Frost

The young psychology teacher, brooding over his inability to make a success of his life, paused for a moment at the side of the old logging road he had been following through the forest. The quiet, familiar beauty of the New Hampshire woods served to ease somewhat the feeling of frustration dogging him, and he was relieved for the moment from thinking about his disappointing efforts to find satisfaction in farming or teaching. Only one vocation really appealed to him—poetry—but at the age of thirty-eight he had yet to sell or publish a single line of verse.

Then it happened. In the distance there suddenly appeared the figure of a man walking toward him. Never before, in countless hikes through the remote area, had he ever chanced to meet another human being, so he watched with interest. As the man drew closer the young teacher observed that his manner and dress were strangely like his own, and for several moments he had the disconcerting feeling that he was somehow looking at himself. The stranger, now well within hailing distance, stopped suddenly at a fork in the road, looked thoughtfully in each direction, and then disappeared as he turned to follow a seldom-traveled path that led deeper into the heart of the woods. Some minutes after the stranger had gone, the would-be poet realized that a decision had been made—a decision to take the road "less traveled." Returning to Teachers College in Plymouth, New Hampshire, he gave notice that he was going to resign. Shortly thereafter, he moved with his family to England.

In 1914, two years later, things were very different. Eager publishers had accepted his poetry, and his name was becoming well known in England and the United States. Thinking back to that all-important day in the New Hampshire woods, he was moved to compose the poem that is now one of the classics in American literature: "The Road Not Taken."

Robert Frost (1874–1963), after following in his chosen vocation for half a century, was everywhere acknowledged as one of America's best, and best-loved, poets. The joy and pleasure he has brought to readers would be hard to measure, and it would be difficult to estimate how many lives have been touched by his wisdom. He never learned the name of the stranger—if indeed there was one—but that is not important. It was Frost himself who took the road "less traveled by," and that "made all the difference." Adventuring spirits will find that the road is still open.

EPILOGUE

Among the many short and simple parting benedictions, our family favorite is the single word, "Mizpah," taken from Genesis 31:49. We use the word itself to convey the benediction drawn from the verse (KJV):

> The LORD watch between me and thee,
> when we are absent one from another.

> *MIZPAH*

WORKS CONSULTED

To list all of the sources for this material, which has been taken from 750 newspaper columns written from 1958 to 1971, would require a library. However, the main reference volumes used are listed below.

The Abingdon Bible Commentary. New York: Abingdon Press, 1929.

Allen, Alexander V. G. *Christian Institutions.* New York: Charles Scribner's Sons, 1916.

American Heritage. 185 vols. New York: Forbes, Inc., 1959–1991.

The Book of Days. Vols. 1 and 2. London and Edinburgh: W. & R. Chambers, Ltd., 1886.

Clark, C. P. S. *Everyman's Book of Saints.* Oxford: A. R. Mowbray & Co., 1956.

The Encyclopaedia Britannica. 29 vols. Cambridge: Cambridge University Press, 1910.

Webster's New Biographical Dictionary. Springfield, Mass.: Merriam-Webster, 1983.

Acknowledgment is also made for sources used for "Bill's Miracle" and "The Contribution of a Freed Slave":

Alcoholics Anonymous, 3d ed. New York: Alcoholics Anonymous World Services, Inc., 1939, pp. 59–60. Reprinted with permission.

Yates, Elizabeth. *Amos Fortune, Free Man.* New York: Puffin Books, 1989.

In addition, the readers and editors of the *San Francisco Examiner, The Grass Valley–Nevada City Union,* and the *Lodi* (Calif.) *News Sentinel* have been very helpful in submitting ideas and information that have been useful in the writing of this book.